LEARNING A LIVING:
A BLUEPRINT FOR HIGH PERFORMANCE

A SCANS REPORT FOR
AMERICA 2000

THE SECRETARY'S COMMISSION ON ACHIEVING NECESSARY SKILLS
U.S. DEPARTMENT OF LABOR
APRIL 1992

★

For sale by the U.S. Government Printing Office
Superintendent of Documents, Mail Stop: SSOP, Washington, DC 20402-9328
ISBN 0-16-037908-3

CONTENTS

EXHIBITS

SIDEBARS

April 1992

The Honorable Lynn Martin
Secretary of Labor
Washington, D.C.

Dear Madam Secretary:

On behalf of my colleagues on the Secretary of Labor's Commission on Achieving Necessary Skills (SCANS), I am pleased to transmit our final report, *Learning a Living: A Blueprint for High Performance.*

In June 1991 this Commission produced *What Work Requires of Schools*, a document defining the workplace competencies and foundation skills required for effective job performance today and tomorrow. Events since then have confirmed our conviction that this know-how is essential for all Americans.

The national self-examination about education and training has continued. The National Education Goals Panel issued its first report card on the goals agreed to by President Bush and the nation's governors in 1989. The President announced *Job Training 2000*, a new effort to improve the job training system. The New American Schools Development Corporation (NASDC) moved forward with its plans to create "break the mold" schools. And the National Council on Education Standards and Testing endorsed the workplace competencies defined by SCANS, suggesting that they be integrated into national standards and assessments of core academic subjects.

The SCANS message, in short, was not delivered in a vacuum but in the midst of an intense national debate about education and training, their purposes, and the progress to date. Each of these efforts has a different focus, and all of them recognize that schools do more than prepare young people for work. But these efforts are all of a piece—elements in a broad nationwide effort to link education to the real world. All seek a particular kind of learner, one who can put knowledge and skills into practice as a productive worker, a responsible citizen, and a more complete human being.

This document completes SCANS' contribution to the conversation. It is in two parts. Part I, Learning a Living, describes the economic choices facing the United States, defines the workforce issue as we understand it, and makes several recommendations to set the nation on the path to a high-performance future. Part I outlines the SCANS vision, describes how schools and the private sector can cooperate to create a high-performance economy capable of maintaining the nation's standard of living, and offers suggestions on how to proceed. In particular, it recommends that, as Secretary of Labor, you take steps to assure support for the continued development of the SCANS agenda.

But visions and recommendations, for all their value, must take root and flower in real schools and workplaces. Part II, A Blueprint for High Performance, provides a more detailed roadmap for those charged with the responsibility for the Commission's major concerns: educators, employers, and the designers of our certification and assessment systems.

This, the SCANS final report, thus hopes to contribute to improving the nation's productivity and the well-being of its citizens in the next century. It moves beyond our previous description of *what* must be done to build high-performance workplaces and schools to a description of *how* we can prepare our young people, as well as those workers already on the job, for productive work in the 21st century.

I know that I speak for all of my Commission colleagues in expressing my admiration for your outstanding support of this effort and for your leadership of the Department responsible for the health, safety, and well-being of the working men and women of America.

Respectfully,

William E. Brock
Chairman

Edward Aguirre
Aguirre International

J. Veronica Biggins
NationsBank

James P. Black
Board of Education
Lauderdale County, Alabama

Charles E. Bradford
International Association of
    Machinists & Aerospace Workers

Patricia L. Brockett
Office of the Governor, Iowa

Walton E. Burdick
International Business Machines

James D. Burge
Motorola, Inc.

Bruce Carswell
GTE Corporation

Thomas W. Chapman
Greater Southeast Healthcare System

Paul F. Cole
New York State AFL/CIO

Gloria J. Conn
Wayne County Regional Educational
    Service Agency

Gabriel Cortina
Los Angeles Unified School District

Frank P. Doyle
General Electric Company

Jay H. Foreman
United Food and Commercial Workers

Badi G. Foster
AEtna Life and Casualty

William H. Gregory
Gregory Forest Products

Yvette Herrera
Communications Workers of America

Madelyn P. Jennings
Gannett Company, Inc.

Steffen E. Palko
Cross Timbers Oil Company

Dale Parnell
Oregon Department of Education

Joan Patterson
UAW/Chrysler National Training Center

Lauren B. Resnick
University of Pittsburgh

Richard E. Rivera
TGI Friday's, Inc.

Roger D. Semerad
RJR Nabisco Foundation

Thomas G. Sticht
Applied Behavioral and Cognitive Sciences, Inc.

Maria Tukeva
Bell Multicultural High School

Gary D. Watts
National Education Association

Sharyn Marr Wetjen
High School Redirection

Gerald Whitburn
Wisconsin Department of Health and Social Services

John H. Zimmerman
MCI Communications

PREFACE

The Secretary's Commission on Achieving Necessary Skills (SCANS) was asked to define the know-how needed in the workplace and to consider how this know-how is best assessed. The Commission was also asked to look to ways to disseminate its findings. The latter mission was expressed best by Secretary Martin in stating that the result of our efforts should not be a report that ended up gathering dust on already overladen shelves but should be, rather, an action plan for schools and workplaces.

The Commission issued its first report in July 1991. That report defined the five competencies and three-part foundation that constitute workplace know-how. That report, *What Work Requires of Schools*, also invited the public to join in the conversation with the Commission.

Since then the SCANS office has received over 20,000 phone calls or letters asking for and giving information. Some 100,000 reports, 200,000 *Executive Summaries*, and 200,000 *Letters to Parents, Employers, and Educators* have been distributed. The public has overwhelmingly supported the know-how definition, but the public also asked questions that have to be answered:

- Why should we change the schools? Wouldn't it be better to reestablish the standards of 30 or 40 years ago?

- Where will the jobs that need these skills be found? Doesn't the workplace have to change first?

- Will the proposed changes be fair to minorities, who are a growing proportion of the U.S. population?

- What steps have to be taken in the education system?

- What has to change in the world of work?

- What must the Federal Government do?

- How do the SCANS proposals fit with the nation's other education reform efforts and with the economic changes that are transforming the job market?

This, our final report, informed by field research that confirmed the findings of *What Work Requires of Schools*, is our answer to these questions. Part I contains three chapters: Chapter 1 is directed to the question, Why change? The answer, in a nutshell, is because economic change has made the high school diploma and what it represents less of a guarantee of a decent wage. The SCANS know-how, however, is correlated with high wages. Chapter 2 identifies the three parts of the *learning and earning system* that must change: the schools, the workplace, and the assessment system. Chapter 3 contains the principles and recommendations that should guide this change.

Part II, which also contains three chapters, is directed to people responsible for implementing change. Chapter 4 is directed to educators who want to create high-performance schools. Chapter 5 is directed to employers, especially to those who are responsible for human resources. And Chapter 6 is directed to persons who are developing a national system of assessment. Part II is not a detailed roadmap or a rigid prescription. Instead, it contains suggestions based on the experience of those who have taken the first steps toward the high-performance future.

LEARNING A LIVING:
A BLUEPRINT FOR HIGH PERFORMANCE

EXECUTIVE SUMMARY

PRINCIPLES AND RECOMMENDATIONS

The Secretary's Commission on Achieving Necessary Skills (SCANS) was appointed by the Secretary of Labor to determine the skills that our young people need to succeed in the world of work. The Commission's fundamental purpose is to encourage a high-performance economy characterized by high-skill, high-wage employment.

Our primary message to schools is this: Look beyond the schoolhouse to the roles students will play when they leave to become workers, parents, and citizens.

Our message to teachers is this: Look beyond your discipline and your classroom to the other courses your students take, to your community, and to the lives of your students outside school. Help your students connect what they learn in class to the world outside.

Our message to employers is this: Look outside your company and change your view of your responsibilities for human resource development. Your old responsibilities were to select the best available applicants and to retain those you hired. Your new responsibilities must be to improve the way you organize work and to develop the human resources in your community, your firm, and your nation.

We want to state at the outset that the well-being of the nation—and its citizens—is *not* synonymous with economic status. There is much more to life than earning a living, and we want more from schools than productive workers. We want citizens who can discharge the responsibilities that go with living in a democratic society and with being parents. As we said in our first report: "A solid education is its own reward and has value beyond specific skills." We are not talking about turning our high schools into trade schools. Nor do we suggest that schools ignore the beauty of literature and scientific theories or the lessons of history and geography.

SCANS focused on one important aspect of schooling: what we call the "learning a living" system. In 1991 SCANS issued its initial report, *What Work Requires of Schools*. As outlined in that report, a high-performance workplace requires workers who have a solid foundation in the basic literacy and computational skills, in the thinking skills necessary to put knowledge to work, and in the personal qualities that make workers dedicated and trustworthy.

But a solid foundation is not enough. High-performance workplaces also require competencies: the ability to manage resources, to work amicably and productively with others, to acquire and use information, to master complex systems, and to work with a variety of technologies. This combination of foundation skills and workplace competencies—"workplace know-how" (see Exhibit 1)—is not taught in many schools or required for most diplomas.

EXHIBIT 1

WORKPLACE KNOW-HOW

The know-how identified by SCANS is made up of five competencies and a three-part foundation of skills and personal qualities that are needed for solid job performance. These are:

WORKPLACE COMPETENCIES: — Effective workers can productively use:

- **Resources**—They know how to allocate time, money, materials, space, and staff.

- **Interpersonal skills**—They can work on teams, teach others, serve customers, lead, negotiate, and work well with people from culturally diverse backgrounds.

- **Information**—They can acquire and evaluate data, organize and maintain files, interpret and communicate, and use computers to process information.

- **Systems**—They understand social, organizational, and technological systems; they can monitor and correct performance; and they can design or improve systems.

- **Technology**—They can select equipment and tools, apply technology to specific tasks, and maintain and troubleshoot equipment.

FOUNDATION SKILLS: — Competent workers in the high-performance workplace need:

- **Basic Skills**—reading, writing, arithmetic and mathematics, speaking, and listening.

- **Thinking Skills**—the ability to learn, to reason, to think creatively, to make decisions, and to solve problems.

- **Personal Qualities**—individual responsibility, self-esteem and self-management, sociability, and integrity.

The time when a high school diploma was a sure ticket to a job is within the memory of workers who have not yet retired; yet in many places today a high school diploma is little more than a certificate of attendance. As a result, employers discount the value of all diplomas, and many students do not work hard in high school.

In fact, the market value of a high school diploma has fallen. The proportion of men between the ages of 25 and 54 with high school diplomas who earn less than enough to support a family of four above the poverty line is growing alarmingly. Among African-American men with 12 years of schooling, the proportion with low earnings rose from 20 percent in 1969 to 42.7 percent in 1989; among Hispanic men, from 16.4 to 35.9 percent; and among white men, from 8.3 percent to 22.6 percent. In other words, in 1989 more than two in five African-American men, one in three Hispanic men, and one in five white men, all with high school diplomas, did not earn enough to lift a family of four above poverty. Unless there is a second earner, their families will not have what most would call a decent living.

The workplace know-how that this Commission has defined is related both to competent performance and to higher earnings for the people who possess it. When the Commission compared the know-how required in 23 high-wage jobs with the requirements of 23 low-wage jobs, the conclusion was inescapable: workers with more know-how command a higher wage—on average, 58 percent, or $11,200 a year, higher.

Everyone must have the opportunity to reach the higher levels of skills and competencies the Commission found to be associated with high-wage jobs. To that end, we have recast the broad principles set forth in *What Work Requires of Schools* as the context for our recommendations:

- **The qualities of high performance that today characterize our most competitive companies must become the standard for the vast majority of our employers, public and private, large and small, local and global.**

- **The nation's schools must be transformed into high-performance organizations.**

- **All Americans should be entitled to multiple opportunities to learn the SCANS know-how well enough to earn a decent living.**

To make those principles a reality we recommend:

1. **The nation's school systems should make the SCANS foundation skills and workplace competencies explicit objectives of instruction at all levels.**

2. **Assessment systems should provide students and workers with a résumé documenting attainment of the SCANS know-how.**

3. **All employers, public and private, should incorporate the SCANS know-how into all their human resource development efforts.**

4. **The Federal Government should continue to bridge the gap between school and the high-performance workplace, by advancing the SCANS agenda.**

5. **Every employer in America should create its own strategic vision around the principles of the high-performance workplace.**

IMPLEMENTATION

The Commission recognizes that nationwide policies are of little value until they are carried out by people on the front line. Cities such as Fort Worth, Los Angeles, Pittsburgh, Tampa, and Louisville and states such as Florida, Indiana, New York, and Oregon have taken steps to put the broad SCANS principles in place in their school systems at the local and state levels. In the corporate sector, TGI Friday's, MCI, Gannett, Motorola, NationsBank, and AT&T (and its major unions) are taking action. A number of trade organizations in the hospitality field have joined together to introduce the SCANS language into their industry. The U.S. Department of Labor is moving to build SCANS into various aspects of Job Training Partnership Act programs. The Federal Government's Office of Personnel Management (OPM) is seeking ways to apply SCANS findings in skills centers for Federal employees.

These leaders and those who follow them can begin the systemic change to a high-performance future. In the process they will have to reinvent education, reorganize work and work-based learning, and restructure educational assessment.

REINVENTING K-12 EDUCATION

During the 1980s the United States, seeking to improve public schools, tried to get more results through tighter curricula, higher certification standards for teachers, and more testing of everyone. Despite the effort, students were performing essentially no better at the end of the decade than they were at the beginning. More of the same was not a successful strategy.

As this Commission argued in *What Work Requires of Schools*, American society today requires that elementary and secondary

schools meet drastically different goals. The job now is to bring all students to a level that, in the past, only a small minority reached. Experts universally agree that this job requires reinventing elementary and secondary education.

President Bush and the nation's governors have agreed on a set of six goals for education. These goals have been generally agreed to by state governments, education leaders, and business groups such as the Business Roundtable. The Commission supports all six goals; its recommendations are particularly pertinent to the two goals that refer to preparing youth and adults for productive employment in our competitive economy.

The experience of schools, districts, and states that are advancing toward high-performance schooling provides important lessons for educators wishing to teach the SCANS know-how:

- **Teaching should be offered "in context," that is, students should learn content while solving realistic problems. "Learning in order to know" should not be separated from "learning in order to do."**

- **Improving the match between what work requires and what students are taught requires changing how instruction is delivered and how students learn.**

- **High performance requires a new system of school administration and assessment.**

- **The entire community must be involved.**

The experience of Fort Worth, Texas, with restructuring its instructional program has shown how the SCANS classroom can differ from the traditional classroom. In Fort Worth, the conventions of today's classroom (teacher omniscience, student passivity and isolation, rigid disciplinary borders, and "abstracted" knowledge and facts) are being replaced with sophisticated and more realistic concepts of instruction and learning (the teacher may not know all the answers, students often learn best in groups, and knowledge is related to real problems).

Resources

Of all the resources required for re-inventing schools around the SCANS ends, none are more important than those devoted to teacher training and staff development. Providing training opportunities for instructional staff will be costly, especially if teachers and administrators are to be given the time they need during the school day and summers for training. But teachers, noninstructional staff, and building and school-district administrators need time if they are to:

- Develop new pedagogical skills required to teach in context and to develop active, collaborative learning environments;

- Learn new instructional management skills and use new instructional technologies to develop new ways of interacting with students; and

- Gain experience with the principles of high performance as applied in restructured workplaces.

Emerging instructional technologies promise to revolutionize teaching and learning by enabling teachers and students to change their traditional roles. When technology dispenses information, teachers are free to coach and facilitate student learning. With technology monitoring learning, students can become active learners, working to acquire new skills.

The SCANS competencies cannot be widely taught unless teachers have instructional materials: textbooks and other print materials, and computer-based and multimedia materials. Video and multimedia materials are essential to creating the realistic contexts in which the competencies are used.

Equity and Diversity

The changes advocated by the Commission promise great benefits to minority and low-income Americans. One-third of new entrants into the American labor force are members of minority groups; they are entitled to an education that will let them learn and will equip them to find and hold a decent job. Because children vary, not only as individuals but also as members of different cultural, racial, and ethnic groups, education must take into account three basic elements that contribute to this diversity:

1. Differences in family income,

2. Limited English-speaking proficiency (LEP), and

3. Differences in learning styles.

Variation and diversity are not the enemies of high-quality education. The enemy is rigid insistence on a factory model of schooling, a prescription for failure that refuses to accommodate diversity or to allow those students with special strengths to function productively.

REORGANIZING FOR HIGH-PERFORMANCE WORK AND WORK-BASED LEARNING

Both high-performance workplaces and highly trained workers are needed if we are to build a high-skilled, high-wage economy. Reinventing K-12 education is necessary but not sufficient because about 80 percent of the workers on whom American employers will depend as we enter the 21st century are already on the job. To create high-performance workplaces, employers must actively work to develop the skills and competence of these workers. Only in this way can they constantly improve the quality of the goods and services they provide and satisfy their customers' needs.

Every American employer, public or private, large or small, local or global, must consider the human resources needed for high performance and high quality. Yet, today, American companies do much less training than some of our international competitors; in fact, fewer than 10 percent of front-line American workers now receive training of any kind.

The Commission believes that employer-sponsored training, both public and private, must be upgraded and organized around the SCANS know-how. As a useful first step, coalitions of trade associations, business organizations, labor unions, and industry-specific groups could develop training strategies and materials around the SCANS know-how for use by all businesses, particularly small firms.

Many young people between the ages of 16 to 25 today are frustrated because their high schools talked of English and geometry, but their workplace speaks a different language. In a system that serves people beyond high school, employers would describe job requirements in terms of the SCANS workplace competencies and use these for recruitment and employee development. Human resource and training managers would reorient their education and training offerings to include not only job-specific skills but also the SCANS workplace competencies and foundation skills.

Providers of education—vocational schools, proprietary schools, community colleges, adult education, and work-based programs—would offer instruction and certification in SCANS workplace competencies. Referral agencies—job counselors in high schools, in employment agencies and the Employment Service, or in the skill centers newly recommended by the Administration—would assess their clients' SCANS workplace competencies, understand job and educational requirements and opportunities in the same terms, and refer clients to career-enhancing work and education.

RESTRUCTURING EDUCATIONAL ASSESSMENT

A system for assessing and certifying the SCANS workplace know-how is essential. If employers and colleges pay attention to the SCANS foundation skills and workplace competencies, students will work to acquire them. If teachers have to certify that the know-how is acquired, they will make the effort to teach it. If parents and community groups understand the standards that graduates are expected to attain, they will demand that their children reach these levels.

The Commission supports the emerging national consensus calling for a new, nationwide, voluntary assessment system. The Commission believes the system should incorporate new techniques of judging performance—not "tests" as traditionally understood, but assessment tied to learning goals. The National Council on Education Standards and Testing has endorsed the inclusion of the SCANS workplace competencies in the system it recommended, stating that the SCANS competencies "can and should be integrated into the national standards and assessments."[1] The Commission hopes that the curriculum development work of several groups—the National Council of Teachers of Mathematics, the National Council of Teachers of English, the National Science Teachers Association, and others—will follow this advice.

The Commission believes that a national system, as recommended by the National Council on Education Standards and Testing, should integrate assessment of proficiency in SCANS know-how with other equally important outcomes of schooling. Such a system is needed to:

- Communicate world-class standards of curriculum content and student performance, and

- Certify individual performance and thereby motivate students and their teachers to meet these standards.

The challenge is to design a system that clearly establishes that all young people in our nation have the right to an education up to a recognized performance standard—without putting the burden of failure on students' backs.

The Commission suggests establishing for all students, beginning in middle school, a cumulative résumé. The résumé would contain information about courses taken, projects completed, and proficiency levels attained in each competency. A student who accomplishes enough to meet an overall standard would be awarded a certificate of initial mastery (CIM), a universally recognized statement of experience and accomplishment. The information would mean the same thing to everybody: this person has the SCANS workplace know-how noted here.

Students would be free to use their résumés in seeking employment or further education at any time. Employers could be expected to demand from students the highest level of certification that the job demands (i.e., high-performance workplaces can demand high skills including, but not limited to, those required for the CIM). It would be up to the consumers of this information—employers, col-

---

[1]*Raising Standards on American Education* (Washington, D.C.: National Council on Education Standards and Testing, January 1992).

leges, the military, or others—to decide what weight to give each element in the résumé, using their own needs and criteria as guides.

In addition to the education-based assessment, a way to assess and certify persons who are already in the workforce (an experience-based assessment) is needed. The Federal Government, some private firms, and a coalition of trade associations in the hospitality industry have begun the hard work that will lead to the needed assessment tools.

IMPROVING THE "LEARNING A LIVING" SYSTEM

The Commission understands that preparation for work is only part of the mission of schools, and that school is only part of the learning process. President Bush has spoken of the need for America to be a nation of learners and for the "education revolution" to extend beyond the schools into the community. This report is concerned with those parts of education and work that form the "learning a living" system.

In the learning-a-living system all students, at least through the second year of high school, learn the SCANS know-how in English, math, science, history, and geography, in other classes (e.g., art), and in extracurricular activities. That is, all students follow a common academic program, a single track, until they are about 16. After age 16, some students are more likely to be learning the SCANS know-how in the context of work, perhaps by specializing in the application of the competencies to a particular industry, such as manufacturing or hospitality.

Some of these students will go on to community colleges in a 2+2 tech-prep program, a program that begins with the last two years of high school and leads to an associate degree after two years of college. Other students will continue to learn the SCANS know-how in academic courses as they move toward a four-year college program. Others will, after graduating, go directly to work and work-based learning.

In addition to formal schooling, learning takes place through employers and work-based education. This learning should continue for a lifetime, supported by the human resource functions of recruiting, developing, and retaining employees. Workplace education produces portable certificates that are valued in many workplaces.

Information should flow from employers to educators through recruiting and employee development activities, including the ways in which employees progress up career ladders. Educators, in turn, should inform employers of the workplace competencies that students have attained. Today, neither employers nor educators receive or deliver information effectively. The SCANS aim is to improve the information flow (and the learning and earning) so that the economy will deliver the high productivity and wage increases that characterized the United States in the years from 1937 to 1973.

Exhibit 2 outlines the actions that are needed to reach the SCANS goals. Unless the nation takes forceful action on this agenda, the nation's schools, employers, students, and workers will not fare well in the next century.

This, the SCANS final report, provides a blueprint for groups at the national, state, and local levels. Each community must decide what

EXHIBIT 2

RECOMMENDATIONS FOR THE "LEARNING A LIVING" SYSTEM

THE COMMISSION RECOMMENDS FULL IMPLEMENTATION OF THE FOLLOWING ACTIONS BY THE YEAR 2000:

Reinventing Schools

- Workplace know-how (the SCANS foundation and workplace competencies) should be taught along the entire continuum of education, from kindergarten through college.

- Every student should complete middle school (about age 14) with an introduction to workplace know-how.

- Every student by about age 16 should attain initial mastery of the SCANS know-how.

- Every student should complete high school sufficiently proficient in the SCANS know-how to earn a decent living.

- All federally funded programs for youth and adults, including vocational education programs, should teach the SCANS know-how.

Fostering Work-Based Learning

- Federal, state, and local agencies should incorporate SCANS workplace competencies into their own employee programs.

- Private-sector work-based training programs should incorporate training in the SCANS workplace competencies.

- Coalitions of businesses, associations, government employers, and labor organizations should teach the SCANS competencies to the current workforce, including employees of small businesses.

Reorganizing the Workplace

- The vast majority of employers should adopt the standards of quality and high performance that now characterize our most competitive companies.

- Firms should develop internal training programs to bring employees to the proficiency in the SCANS competencies needed for high-performance work organizations.

Restructuring Assessment

- A national education-based assessment system should be implemented that will permit educational institutions to certify the levels of the SCANS competencies that their students have achieved.

- Public and private employers should define requirements for higher-level competencies.

- Employment-based assessments should permit diagnoses of individual learning needs.

---

resources will be allocated to create a system that will meet its specific goals. But first, each must become involved in a conversation about its place in a fast-changing world as we approach the year 2000. Our nation's ability to lead in a global economy will depend on the outcome of those conversations. This Commission is confident that once they are informed, communities will commit themselves to maintaining the American dream for themselves and their children.

PART I

LEARNING
A LIVING

Chapter 1
TIME TO DECIDE

About 150 years ago a French visitor named Alexis de Tocqueville described the United States as a "land of wonders" in which "what is not yet done is only what [they have] not yet attempted to do." Through the generations the people of the United States have proudly lived up to that description. American ingenuity and creativity expanded the frontiers of technology. Our science and engineering took men and women into space. And American know-how gave the United States pride of place in the world's economy.

Ingenuity, creativity, hard work, and know-how made the American dream come true for millions of our citizens. Much of the rest of the world is now trying to live it. The dream is that the standard of living of each new generation will exceed that of their parents. Holding fast to that dream in the United States is what this document is all about, because today this "land of wonders" is being tested anew.

For most of this century, America took its goods to the world without worrying about competition from abroad. The quality of our goods and services was second to none. American production techniques and know-how were the envy of the world. American markets, isolated by two great oceans, belonged to American producers. Those days are behind us.

Today, telecommunications and modern air transportation have created a truly global vil-lage. More than 70 percent of American manu-factured products are subject to competition from abroad. The globalization of finance, capi-tal, technology, and labor means that a product can be designed in one country, engineered in another, produced in yet a third, and distributed around the world. If the next generation of Americans is to enjoy the increasing economic prosperity that blessed the post-World War II generation, the United States must be prepared to respond to these challenges.

Internationally, competitive pressure on the American economy can only increase. As a new century approaches, Europe will be eco-nomically united for the first time in history. Its huge market will stretch from the North Sea to the Mediterranean, from Ireland to what used to be called the Iron Curtain. The countries of Eastern Europe and the new members of the Commonwealth of Independent States will struggle in fits and starts to develop market-based economies. Japan and other newly indus-trialized Asian nations will continue to succeed.

If we are to respond effectively, trade agreements must give all parties a fair chance to compete. Barriers to American products overseas must be diminished. The private sec-tor must invest more in our country's plants, equipment, and technology. Yet none of these will be sufficient without urgent and effective action to improve the productivity and skills of our workforce—the central concern of SCANS. We are concerned both with preparing young people still in school and with upgrading the skills of people already in the workforce.

However, this concern must not be misinterpreted. We want to state at the outset that the well-being of the nation—and of its citizens—is *not* synonymous with economic status. There is much more to life than earning a living, and we want more from education than productive workers. We want citizens who can discharge the responsibilities that go with living in a democratic society and with becoming parents. As we said in our first report: "A solid education is its own reward and has value beyond specific skills." We are not talking about transforming high schools into trade schools that ignore the beauty of literature, the elegance of scientific theories, or the lessons of history and geography. To quote a comment made after the first SCANS report:

> SCANS calls for a revival of the ancient and honorable idea of a liberal education, the education that makes lives of ordered liberty possible. Writing more than 150 years ago in *The Uses of University*, John Henry Newman captured the essence of the SCANS report when he said that the only truly vocational education is a liberal education.[1]

Workplace productivity, however, is the key to national wealth and earning a decent living is important to most of us. America is the world's wealthiest nation because its workers are the world's most productive. But America no longer leads the world in productivity *increases*, that is, in the extra amount produced per worker each year. In the last generation, American productivity has grown at a snail's pace, dropping from an average growth rate of 3 percent a year between 1937 and 1973 to less than 1 percent since 1973. Over the past 20 years, wealth for both families and the nation was increased by putting more people, particularly more women, to work, but we can no longer sustain that strategy.

Clearly, all of us—as individuals, communities, employers, and a nation—have reached a point of decision. We can choose between raising productivity through a conscious effort to build an equitable, high-skill, high-wage future, or we can ignore the productivity side of the economic equation by settling for a low-skill, low-wage economy and its inevitable accompaniment, declining standards of living for most.[2] We dare not choose badly.

A HIGH-PERFORMANCE ECONOMY

To choose well is to go on the offensive. The SCANS goal is a high-performance economy—one characterized by high skills, high wages, and full employment—in which every human being's resources are put to their best use. The high-performance workplace is one that empowers workers to participate and utilize fully their skills and knowledge. The future we

[1]Denis P. Doyle, "Focusing on Education," *Atlantic Monthly* (October 1991).

[2]*America's Choice: High Skills or Low Wages!* (Rochester, N.Y.: National Center on Education and the Economy (NCEE), June 1990).

want for our country and our children leads us inevitably in this direction.

A blue-ribbon Commission on Industrial Productivity noted in 1989:

> In the course of its work the Commission discovered many American firms that are thriving in the new economic climate and indeed are leading the way in international competition. The success of those firms suggests a vision of a new industrial America, a nation equipped to exploit the best ideas and innovations from abroad as well as its own inherent strengths.[3]

The characteristics of these high-performance workplaces are easy enough to spot, though difficult to achieve:

- Flexible and decentralized production techniques;

- Employee empowerment, by giving employees decision-making responsibility, career paths, and wage progression tied to skills;

- A strong emphasis on "excellence," on continuously improving work performance, and on the kind of management for quality that reduces error and rework, increases customer satisfaction, and cuts costs;

- Continual training to upgrade skills and employees' ability to function effectively in a problem-oriented environment; and

- Increasing integration of tasks through work teams and the identification of workers with their products and services.

What Work Requires of Schools was the first SCANS contribution to the high-performance discussion. It created a common vocabulary to help the worlds of work and school to communicate. Despite the widespread agreement among employers and educators that too many young people complete school unequipped for the workplace, there has been no clear communication about what the schools should do. We described educators and business leaders as "ships passing in the night" on this issue.

That report also acknowledged that "schools do more than prepare people to make a living . . . They prepare people to live full lives—to participate in their communities, to raise families, and to enjoy the leisure that is the fruit of their labor." Nevertheless, we must emphasize that schools have an important role to play in moving our nation to a high-performance future.

WORKPLACE KNOW-HOW

This Commission began its task by defining competency in the high-performance workplace. Defining competency led to a major data-gathering effort, in which we talked to hundreds of employers, supervisors, and especially employees across the entire spectrum of the American economy. The SCANS investigation found a clear pattern of requirements. A high-performance workplace demands workers who have a solid foundation in the traditional basic academic skills, in the thinking skills necessary

---

[3]Michael L. Dertouzos, Richard K. Lester, and Robert M. Solow, *Made in America: Regaining the Productive Edge* (Cambridge, Mass.: MIT Press, 1989).

to put knowledge to work, and in the personal characteristics that make a worker confident, trustworthy, and responsible. We called this the "foundation" of workplace know-how.

But a solid foundation is not enough. High-performance workplaces also require the ability to manage resources, to work amicably and productively with others, to acquire and use information, to understand and master complex systems, and to work comfortably with a variety of technologies. We called these the "competencies."

Workplace know-how is a combination of the foundation skills and the workplace competencies (see Exhibit A). The competencies cannot be achieved without the foundation; but the two can—and should—be learned simultaneously. The know-how is not taught in most high schools or required for most diplomas.

The day when a high school diploma was a sure job ticket is within the memory of workers who have not yet retired. In many places today, however, a high school diploma is

EXHIBIT A

WORKPLACE KNOW-HOW

The know-how identified by SCANS is made up of five competencies and a three-part foundation of skills and personal qualities that are needed for solid job performance. These are:

WORKPLACE COMPETENCIES:— Effective workers can productively use:

- **Resources**—They know how to allocate time, money, materials, space, and staff.

- **Interpersonal skills**—They can work on teams, teach others, serve customers, lead, negotiate, and work well with people from culturally diverse backgrounds.

- **Information**—They can acquire and evaluate data, organize and maintain files, interpret and communicate, and use computers to process information.

- **Systems**—They understand social, organizational, and technological systems; they can monitor and correct performance; and they can design or improve systems.

- **Technology**—They can select equipment and tools, apply technology to specific tasks, and maintain and troubleshoot equipment.

FOUNDATION SKILLS:— Competent workers in the high-performance workplace need:

- **Basic Skills**—reading, writing, arithmetic and mathematics, speaking, and listening.

- **Thinking Skills**—the ability to learn, to reason, to think creatively, to make decisions, and to solve problems.

- **Personal Qualities**—individual responsibility, self-esteem and self-management, sociability, and integrity.

EXHIBIT B

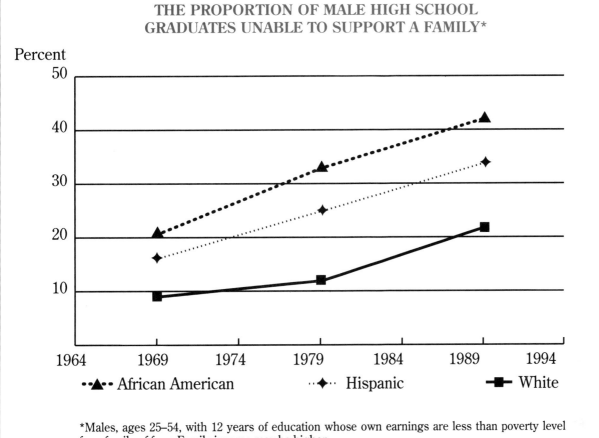

THE PROPORTION OF MALE HIGH SCHOOL GRADUATES UNABLE TO SUPPORT A FAMILY*

Percent

· ▲ · African American   **··◆·· Hispanic**   **■ White**

*Males, ages 25–54, with 12 years of education whose own earnings are less than poverty level for a family of four. Family income may be higher.

Source: Sheldon Danziger, "The Poor," in David Hornbeck and Lester Salamon., *Human Capital and America's Future* (Baltimore: Johns Hopkins Press, 1991), p. 148, and unpublished data for 1989.

little more than a certificate of attendance. As a result, employers discount the value of all diplomas, and students do not work hard in school.

As Exhibit B shows, the market value of a high school diploma is falling. The proportion of men between the ages of 25 and 54 with high school diplomas who earn less than enough to support a family of four above the poverty line is growing alarmingly.[4] Among African-American men with 12 years of schooling, the proportion with low earnings rose from 20 percent in 1969 to 42.7 percent in 1989; among Hispanic men, from 16.4 to 35.9 percent; and among white men from 8.3 percent to 22.6 per-

---

[4]Data on women in the workforce, relating their educational levels to earnings, are not reliable over the same time period because the participation of women in the world of work changed so dramatically.

cent. Unless there is a second earner, their families will not have what most would call a decent living. What these figures mean is that the American dream has turned into a hollow promise for many people, especially those who do not go to college. For some, their high school diploma has become a ticket to underemployment or unemployment. In the words of *What Work Requires of Schools,* "They face bleak prospects—dead-end work, interrupted only by periods of unemployment, with little chance to climb a career ladder."

CHICKEN OR EGG?

Many people have asked, Is there really a skills shortage? Is the high-performance workplace a reality? More to the point from the SCANS perspective, Is the know-how we have defined really related to job performance and to rewards for competent performance? These are thoughtful, legitimate questions. What is the evidence?

The growing wage premium between workers with college degrees and those with only a high school diploma is a powerful sign that more knowledge and skills are in relatively high demand. Too often, however, employers are turning to college graduates to obtain skills that, in other nations, are found in high school graduates.

What previously has been only anecdotal evidence regarding a skills shortage is now being confirmed by surveys. In a recent survey by the National Association of Manufacturers, for example, employers reported that they had to interview six applicants to find one qualified employee. One-quarter of the companies said they could not improve product quality because employees were not capable of learning appropriate skills. About 30 percent complained of being unable to install modern work systems because employees could not learn new jobs.[5]

Nevertheless, commentators on the previous SCANS report thought we had overstated our case when we reported that "more than half our young people leave school without the knowledge or foundation required to find and hold a good job." America's economy, they argued, is not nearly so far along in developing high-performance workplaces that there is a skill shortage; indeed, there is more likely to be a shortage of good jobs. Other commentators asked, Which comes first: do highly skilled workers enable their employers to develop a high-performance workplace, or do employers first create such workplaces and then look for the right kind of worker?

This is a classic chicken-and-egg argument. It can be resolved only by recognizing that *both* high-performance workplaces and highly trained workers are needed.[6] Whatever their order, each reinforces the other, and the absence of either can retard the other's development, ultimately weakening the nation and slow-

---

[5]William Kolberg and Foster Smith, "Our Unsung Olympic Hero," *Washington Post* (February 23, 1991).

[6]Arnold Packer and John Wirt, "Restructuring Work and Learning," in George Peterson and Wayne Vroman, *Urban Labor Markets and Job Opportunities* (Washington, D.C.: Urban Institute, in press).

ly lowering Americans' standard of living. What remains true is that firms cannot organize for a truly competitive and productive future around skills they cannot find. Conversely, students contemplating work will not be motivated to develop new skills unless employers value those skills.

Is the SCANS know-how related to higher wages? In addition to defining the skills needed for employment, the Commission collected task descriptions from workers and supervisors interviewed during the SCANS research.[7] We later rated examples of specific job tasks associated with each of the SCANS skills on a scale of difficulty from 1 (low) to 5 (high). Exhibit C compares the know-how required in 23 high-wage jobs with the know-how requirements of 23 low-wage jobs. The conclusion is inescapable: On average, workers with high levels of know-how, as measured on the 1-to-5 scale, command a weekly wage 58 percent higher than people with lower levels of the skills. Workers in the high-wage jobs received an average weekly wage of $513; those in the low-wage jobs, $298.[8]

On an annual basis, the average difference is impressive. It amounts to about $11,200, enough for a down payment on a new house, a year of a child's college education, or a moderately priced new car. SCANS know-how pays off, for individuals, for families, and for the larger economy.

Bringing the SCANS know-how to everyone will necessarily involve all of American education, K-12 and beyond, including colleges, trade and vocational schools, businesses, and trade associations. Whether they proceed directly to work, apprenticeship, the armed services, or further education, all young Americans should complete high school with the know-how they need to make their way in the world. Within current efforts to restructure education, the Commission wants to identify what has to be done to teach the SCANS know-how. There are no proven blueprints because no nation has ever before attempted such an effort. Yet, in the words of Tocqueville, what Americans have not yet done is only what they have not yet attempted to do. The task we outline will not be accomplished easily or soon. But it must be done—and done well.

---

[7] The Commission interviewed about 200 people. The sample was not a scientifically valid cross section of the American workforce.

[8] The SCANS research involved 50 jobs. For this particular analysis they were divided into 25 high-wage and 25 low-wage jobs. Four jobs did not fit the Bureau of Labor Statistics (BLS) classification scheme and were deleted, leaving two job groups with 23 jobs apiece. High-wage jobs (e.g., programming technicians) paid between $374 and $654 a week; low-wage jobs (e.g., child-care aide) paid between $203 and $373 a week. Data on which Exhibit C is based can be found in *Skills and Tasks for Jobs: A SCANS Report for America 2000* (Washington, D.C.: U.S. Department of Labor, 1992). See Appendix C.

EXHIBIT C

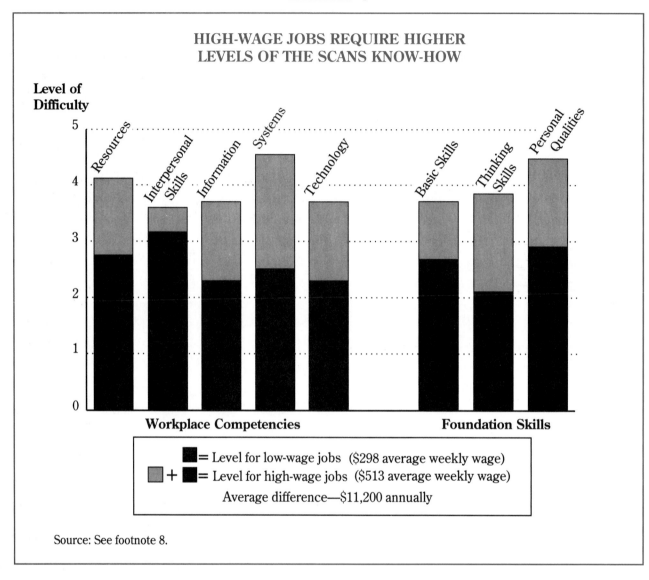

**HIGH-WAGE JOBS REQUIRE HIGHER
LEVELS OF THE SCANS KNOW-HOW**

Level of Difficulty

Workplace Competencies: Resources, Interpersonal Skills, Information, Systems, Technology

Foundation Skills: Basic Skills, Thinking Skills, Personal Qualities

■ = Level for low-wage jobs ($298 average weekly wage)

▨ + ■ = Level for high-wage jobs ($513 average weekly wage)

Average difference—$11,200 annually

Source: See footnote 8.

Chapter 2
SOLVING THE SKILLS PROBLEM

The ability of a workforce to make the best of new technologies may be a country's best competitive advantage. . . To change it, governments need to start at the school gates.

—*The Economist*[9]

A world-class economy requires a world-class workforce. We cannot have the former without the latter. The economic evidence is clear: a significant proportion of productivity growth in the United States earlier this century depended on the growing skills of the workforce.[10] The Commission concludes that in recent years the United States' ability to grow has been hampered because its human resource base is badly in need of upgrading.

REORGANIZING THE WORKPLACE

In a world where routine production and services are up for grabs globally and hundreds of millions of workers overseas are happy to work for less than American workers, our main hope for competitive advantage lies in the value our workforce can add in terms of quality, flexibility, and customization. The game has changed. American workers and managers cannot win playing by the old rules. Rule one was that the boss was always right. Rule two was that employees did what they were told. And rule three was that companies should standardize production because profitability depended on producing more and selling it more cheaply, what experts call "economies of scale." There were plenty of other rules—each a variation of these three—all designed to support standardized production in enormous volume, a factory model of work based on the research of Frederick Taylor.[11]

The old workplace could not use, and in fact did not want, too much creativity or ingenuity among the workforce. A small number of people acted as decision makers—gathering and sifting information, setting up systems, organizing workflow and office arrangements, manipulating data to solve problems, and, above all, handing out orders to govern the minute-to-minute actions of employees. For this old workplace, the public schools were ideal. The schools did a magnificent job of turning out just the kind of product required. Workers needed

[9]"Innovation," *The Economist* (January 11, 1992), p. 19.

[10]Edward F. Denison, *Trends in American Economic Growth, 1929-1982* (Washington, D.C.: Brookings Institution, 1985). His analysis indicates that education was directly responsible for about 27 percent of all growth in output per worker between the Depression years and the 1980s. Another 44 percent of productivity growth was attributed to new knowledge, that is, the combination of education, research, development, and new inventions and technologies.

[11]Frederick W. Taylor, *The Principles of Scientific Management* (New York: W.W. Norton, 1967).

enough education to read, write, and comprehend instructions. Above all they needed to follow instructions faithfully and show up for work reliably.

But in the emerging high-performance workplace virtually everyone acts as a decision maker, gathers and sifts information, sets up and troubleshoots systems, organizes workflow and team arrangements, manipulates data to solve problems, and, on occasion, provides directions to colleagues. Modern work is just too complex for a small cadre of managers to possess all the answers. Consider automobile repair as an example: It has been estimated that in 1965 a mechanic who understood about 500 pages of various repair manuals could fix just about any car on the road. Today the same mechanic would need nearly 500,000 pages of manuals, the equivalent of about 50 New York City telephone books.

REINVENTING EDUCATION

The SCANS thesis is that schools must also become high-performance workplaces. That is where SCANS' workplace know-how comes in. The schools must teach it, and, furthermore, must ensure that all graduates possess it. Despite the widespread public outcry about deficiencies in school preparation, this Commission was able to find only limited evidence that educational institutions are taking this new high-performance path.

The educational reforms of the 1980s demonstrated that it is futile to try to wring high performance from schools by doing more of the same—more tests, more classes, and more

time, thus playing the old school game with more of the old rules.

The new game requires new rules. A process of educational invention is required to restructure schools around teaching the SCANS foundation skills and competencies so that "learning to do" is integrated with "learning to know." The experience of schools, districts, and states that are breaking new ground in advancing high-performance schooling is described more fully in Chapter 4. These pioneers provide important lessons:

- **Teaching should be offered in context. "Learning in order to know" should not be separated from "learning in order to do."**

- **Improving the match between what work requires and what students are taught requires changing how instruction is delivered and how students learn.**

- **High-performance requires a new system of school administration and assessment.**

- **The entire community must be involved.**

SCANS believes that applying these lessons will free up the schools to teach new skills in new ways. It insists that students need not first learn in the abstract what they will later be expected to apply. It considers students as workers in the learning enterprise, not as buckets waiting to be filled. It liberates teachers to develop new pedagogical and instructional skills.

Equity and Diversity

The changes advocated by this Commission promise great benefits to minority and low-income Americans. The increasing number of high school graduates with lower earnings, as was shown by Exhibit B, demonstrates that many are poorly served today. But in a high-performance economy nobody can be left out. In the "production model" organization of schooling, many minority and low-income youngsters are passed through the system, rarely challenged, only to discover too late that lack of genuine achievement bars further progress. The reinvented schools advocated by SCANS promise to change that situation by establishing clear standards for what all students need to know and be able to do, and then organizing education and work to entitle students to the services they need to meet the standards. For the first time, parents will be armed with the knowledge of what students have to do in order to succeed. They will know how well their youngsters are doing as they move through school.

This agenda is all the more critical as the United States approaches a new century. Already one-third of new entrants into the American labor force are members of minority groups; they are entitled to an education that will provide the skills needed to find and hold a decent job. That objective cannot be accomplished by providing the same educational experience for all. Children vary, not only as individuals but also as members of different cultural, racial, and ethnic groups. Education and training efforts must respond to three basic elements that contribute to this diversity:

1. *Differences in family income.* Children of poverty are an increasing proportion of the school population; and family and community problems place a growing burden on the schools that serve them.[12]

2. *Limited English-speaking proficiency (LEP).* The 1990 census reports a 53 percent growth in Hispanic populations and a 108 percent growth among Asian-minority people in America. Job success requires the SCANS know-how *in English.* Schools must develop these skills in a linguistically and culturally sensitive manner. Teachers must use approaches that respect personal interactions across cultures and cultural patterns of dealing with authority and responding to family obligations.

3. *Differences in learning styles.* Recent cognitive research points to the diversity of styles by which people learn. Education in the SCANS skills must begin with the realization that there are many paths to the same goal; that assessments should play to students' strengths, not their weaknesses; and that tests should not needlessly penalize students who need more time, are unconventional thinkers, or are bored by multiple-choice tests.[13] Schools should keep in mind the many famous people such as Thomas Edison,

---

[12]The work of James Comer at Yale and the activities of organizations such as Cities in the Schools are examples of productive relations between schools and low-income communities that work to sustain learning.

[13]Howard Gardner, *The Unschooled Mind* (New York: Basic Books, 1991), and *Frames of Mind* (New York: Basic Books, 1987).

Gustave Flaubert, Woodrow Wilson, and Nelson Rockefeller, who were initially classified as poor students and went on to great success.[14]

Variation and diversity are not the enemies of high-quality education. The enemy is rigid insistence on a factory model of schooling, a prescription for failure that refuses to accommodate diversity or allow those students with special strengths to function productively.

REDESIGNING WORK-BASED LEARNING

If high-performance workplaces are to become the norm in the United States, the SCANS know-how must also form the foundation of adult education and training programs. More than 80 percent of the people who will be working as the new century dawns are already on the job.

By international standards, most American workers receive very little training. Where American companies concentrate training on their college graduates—and most small firms provide no training at all—major foreign competitors concentrate on developing workplace skills at all levels of the company. About two-thirds of the employed workers in West Germany have completed an apprenticeship program, while the Japanese integrate on-the-job training with day-to-day operations. French,

Korean, Singaporean, and Swedish workers benefit from programs unavailable here.[15]

In the United States the transition from school to work is hit-or-miss, and most work-based training is provided to managers and executives. Less than 10 percent of front-line workers now receive training of any kind. According to a survey by Towers/Perrin for the National Association of Manufacturers (NAM),

- Respondents recognized the need for more training, but were not yet making the needed economic investment.

- Companies were reluctant to evaluate the extent of the skills mismatch in their workforce.

- The level of involvement with remedial training programs and local schools was comparatively low.

- Companies of all sizes were reluctant to deal with skill deficiencies among their workers, although they admitted that these deficiencies cause serious business problems.[16]

This Commission believes that employer-sponsored training, both public and private, must be upgraded and integrated around the SCANS know-how. Moreover, apprenticeship training, and second-chance efforts for the unemployed and marginally employed, should be reoriented to integrate the SCANS skills into their basic education and job-specific training.

---

[14]Sally Smith, *Succeeding Against the Odds* (New York: St. Martin's Press, 1991).

[15]Office of Technology Assessment (OTA), U.S. Congress, *Worker Training: Competing in the New International Economy* (Washington, D.C.: U.S. Government Printing Office, September 1990), pp. 21 and 94.

[16]*Today's Dilemma, Tomorrow's Competitive Edge* (Washington, D.C.: Towers/Perrin Co., November 1991).

RESTRUCTURING ASSESSMENT OF KNOW-HOW

"Will this be on the final?" is a familiar question in American schools. In the absence of a system for assessing and certifying the SCANS know-how, it will not be learned. If employers and colleges pay attention to the SCANS foundation skills and workplace competencies, students will work to acquire them. If teachers have to certify that the workplace competencies are acquired, they will make the effort to teach them. If parents and community groups understand the standards that graduates are expected to attain, they will demand that their children reach these levels.

This Commission supports the emerging national consensus calling for a new, nationwide, voluntary assessment system.[17] The Commission believes that the system should (1) apply both to students and adults, to the classroom and the workplace; (2) incorporate new techniques of judging performance—not "tests" as traditionally understood, but assessment tied to learning goals; and (3) include locally developed assessment tasks.

An education-based system should assess mastery of the SCANS know-how as well as mastery of the traditional academic subjects. The assessment system should:

- Establish clear, high standards of student performance;

- Encourage students to meet the standards by creating a cumulative record of courses taken, projects completed, and assessments of student mastery of both academic subjects and SCANS competencies; and

- Provide a basis for holding the education system and body politic accountable to meet the equity goal of providing all students with sufficient skills to earn a decent living.

In addition to assessing and certifying the progress of students (education-based assessment), there must be a way to assess and certify those who are already in the workforce (experience-based assessment). Thus jobs must be described, workers' capabilities assessed, and training opportunities provided, all in the same terms. The terms are the workplace know-how that was shown in Exhibit A.

[17]*Raising Standards for American Education* (Washington, D.C.: National Council for Education Standards and Testing, January 1992).

★

Chapter 3
TOWARD A HIGH-PERFORMANCE FUTURE

> The single most important thing to remember about any enterprise is that results exist only on the outside. The result of a business is a satisfied customer . . . . The result of a school is a student who has learned something and put it to work ten years later.
> —Peter Drucker[18]

The insight of business expert Peter Drucker is key to the concept of high performance. High performance requires looking beyond one's school, company, or organization. This Commission exists because the Secretary of Labor looked beyond the world of Labor Department programs to the world of schools and workplaces.

Our primary message to schools is this: Look beyond the schoolhouse to the roles students will play when they leave to become workers, parents, and citizens.

To teachers we say this: Look beyond your discipline and your classroom to the other courses your students take, to your community, and to the lives of your students outside school. Help your students connect what they learn in class to the world outside.

To administrators we say this: Try to apply the 14 points shown in Exhibit D. These points were developed by W. Edwards Deming, the man whose ideas produced the Japanese economic miracle and the redirection of American businesses toward quality as the touchstone for productivity growth.[19]

To employers we say: Look outside your company and its costs, to your customers and suppliers, and encourage your employees to look beyond their departments. Most emphatically we say this: Change your view of your responsibilities for human resource development. It is no accident that more than half of Deming's widely admired principles deal directly with human resources, and one speaks directly to the company's training programs. As an employer, your old responsibilities were to select the best available applicants and retain those you hired. Your new responsibilities must include developing the human resources in your community, your firm, and your nation.

For your company's sake, be concerned about the community's schools. The public (or private) school that is not "good enough" for your children will be the source of your employees, your customers, and the employees of your suppliers. For your company's sake, think of the schools as critical to your success. In Deming's

---

[18]*The New Realities* (New York: Harper and Row, 1989).

[19]W. Edwards Deming, *Out of the Crisis* (Cambridge, Mass.: MIT Press, 1982).

EXHIBIT D

DEMING'S 14 POINTS TOWARD QUALITY

1. Create constancy of purpose for improvement of product and service.

2. Management must be responsible for change.

3. Do not depend on mass inspection; build quality into the product.

4. Do not award contracts on the basis of price alone.

5. Improve constantly, and thus constantly decrease costs.

6. Institute training on the job.

7. Supervisors should aim to help people and gadgets do a better job.

8. Drive out fear, so that everyone may work effectively.

9. Break down barriers between departments to make teams.

10. Eliminate slogans and targets for the workforce.

11. Eliminate numerical quotas for the workforce (and management).

12. Remove barriers that rob people of pride of workmanship.

13. Encourage education and self-improvement for everyone.

14. Take action to accomplish the transformation.

terms, you must work with those on whom you depend, cultivating a long-term relationship with them, in order to improve the quality of your goods and services and maintain your position in the market. The quality of today's students will determine the future of your enterprise. Help the schools meet the SCANS requirements, and increase the training and education of persons already in the workforce.

DEFINING HIGH PERFORMANCE

For many people, the 14 points proposed by Deming define high performance. The two key lessons this Commission takes from Deming are these:

1. The more quality—including human resource quality—you build into anything, the less, in the long run, it costs.

2. Leadership in any organization—be it school, company, or government agency—lies primarily in developing constancy of purpose throughout.

By applying these two lessons, Deming helped turn the phrase "Made in Japan" from a mark of derision to a hallmark of quality. The high-performance workplace in America will be developed the same way.

Because of Deming and other experts on quality, the United States is slowly leaving the work world designed by Frederick Taylor early in this century. That world rested on hierarchical organizations in which powerful managers told tightly controlled workers how to do their jobs, broken down into small bits, and how to do them faster and faster. The new vision promises a high-performance economy and greater opportunity and responsibility for managers and workers if they have the skills.

Acceptance of Deming's principles has already created some American miracles. Telecommunications, electronics, and automobile firms have won Baldrige awards for quality.[20] Motorola, for example, has reduced its "defects rate" per million manufactured electronic components from 6,000 to 40, with a target of 3.4 in 1992. One result has been savings in manufacturing costs over five years of $700 million, about 6.4 percent of the company's revenues in 1990. According to recent public accounts, Motorola's operating principles are straightforward:[21]

1. Recognize that quality is in the eye of the customer.

2. Reduce the "learning cycle" for developing new products and getting them "right" the first time.

3. Build redundancy into products to keep quality high.

4. Push responsibility down the ranks of the organization.

RECOMMENDATIONS

Creating high-performance workplaces is not simple, but it must be done. We must give all Americans multiple opportunities to become competent enough to earn their way out of poverty. To these ends, we have recast the broad principles set forth in *What Work Requires of Schools* as the context for our recommendations.

- **The qualities of high performance that today characterize our most competitive companies must become the standard for the vast majority of our employers, public and private, large and small, local and global.**

- **The nation's schools must also be transformed into high-performance organizations.**

- **All Americans should be entitled to multiple opportunities to learn the SCANS know-how well enough to earn a decent living.**

To make those principles a reality we recommend the following:

---

[20]The purpose of the Malcolm Baldrige National Quality Award, signed into Federal law in 1987, is to promote quality awareness, recognize high-quality achievement of U.S. companies, and publicize successful quality strategies. The Secretary of Commerce and the National Institute of Standards and Technology (NIST) administer the award with cooperation and financial help from the private sector. Since its inception, the Baldrige Award has been given to 12 companies, including Motorola and Zytec Corporation for manufacturing, Federal Express for service, and Marlow Industries for small business. The application process for the Baldrige Award is rigorous, and heavy emphasis is placed on high-quality achievement and quality improvement as demonstrated through quantitative data furnished by applicants.

[21]"Future Perfect," *The Economist* (January 4, 1992).

1. **The nation's school systems should make the SCANS foundation skills and workplace competencies explicit objectives of instruction at all levels.**

Research on effective learning validates what every classroom teacher knows from personal experience: the more closely learning is tied to "real world" contexts and consequences, the more profound and durable it becomes. We believe such "learning in context" is essential to acquiring the SCANS know-how. Learning and doing must become a single activity throughout education, from kindergarten through high school and beyond.

This Commission believes that a massive reexamination of teacher training and in-service education is required. We call on all teacher-training institutions, professional associations, curriculum developers, and publishers to begin addressing the changes that teaching the SCANS know-how will require. We believe that this task will eventually involve redefining state curriculum frameworks and certification requirements for teachers and making sweeping overhauls in the texts and other materials—including multimedia and computer-based materials that support learning. It is not too soon to begin.

We urge state and local educators (including administrators, teachers, principals, and school board members) to work with local advisory groups (including management, labor, and community groups) to review pedagogy, curriculum, and the administration of schools for opportunities to advance the SCANS know-how. This review might include the following issues:

- How can the SCANS foundation skills and workplace competencies be taught throughout K-12 education?

- What resources in the form of teacher training, technology, new instructional materials, and school and district reorganization are needed to teach the SCANS know-how?

- How can this school and school system become a high-performance organization?

2. **Assessment systems should provide students with a résumé documenting attainment of the SCANS know-how.**

The current national discussion about standards and assessment is long overdue, but it will be of little use if the skills and competencies required for high-performance work are ignored. It is as important that today's students know how to improve the performance of systems continuously (indeed, to understand what a "system" is) as it is that they know how to think mathematically, write a term paper, or complete an experiment. New nationwide standards and assessments that ignore the SCANS know-how will keep our schools and young people from realizing their full potential.

The Commission is pleased to note that the National Council on Education Standards and Testing has endorsed the inclusion of the SCANS competencies in the system it recommended, stating that they "can and should be integrated into the national standards and assessments."[22] Others have proposed a certificate of initial mastery (CIM) as the linchpin for an assessment of both academic subjects and the SCANS competencies.[23] The Commission believes that such a certificate should be based on student résumés. Beginning in the middle school, a cumulative résumé containing information about courses taken, projects completed, and assessment results should be established for each student. As students meet the standards set for specific skills, that mastery would be noted on the résumé.

In addition, when students have met world-class standards across courses and the SCANS competencies, the résumé should show that they have been awarded the CIM.

As discussed more fully in Chapter 6, this Commission's members believe that assessment grounded in world-class standards can succeed in the United States only if the burden of failure is not borne solely by students. The résumé should certify student mastery of subject matter and the SCANS know-how at world-class levels. Students should be *entitled* to educational services—publicly supported in schools, community service or community-based youth organizations, or privately supported in school or on the job—until they can demonstrate that mastery.

This Commission believes that employers who hire youngsters who do not have the CIM have a special responsibility toward these young men and women. Employers should see to it that such employees are enrolled in second-chance programs or, if appropriate programs are unavailable, should provide the needed work-based training opportunities themselves.

3. **All employers, public and private, should incorporate the SCANS know-how into all their human resource development efforts.**

Much formal education and training occur in the private sector—perhaps $50 billion annually. The private sector should take an active hand in developing the skills and competence of the workers on whom it depends. Specifically, we suggest the following:

- Employers, as well as educators, should use the SCANS language.

- All companies should consider the SCANS know-how in their recruitment and employee-development activities and in their development of position descriptions and compensation plans.

- Human resource and training managers should reorient their education and training offerings to include not only job-specific skills for employees but also the SCANS workplace competencies and foundation skills.

- Coalitions of trade associations, business organizations, labor unions, and industry-specific groups should develop training materials around the SCANS know-how for use with all businesses, particularly small firms.

---

[22]See NCEST, *Raising Standards for American Education.*

[23]See NCEE, *America's Choice.*

- Every American employer or, business, large and small, local or global, should assess itself against the principles of high performance and high quality outlined in this document—and the human resource implication of these principles.

On the theory that "physicians should first heal themselves," one of the first places to begin implementing the SCANS agenda is through the in-house education and training efforts conducted by Federal departments and agencies for their employees. The Office of Personnel Management (OPM), the human resource organization that serves Federal Government agencies, has already taken the first steps. Such foundation skills as listening, speaking, solving problems, and thinking creatively are already a part of much Federal training and could be readily adapted to reflect the SCANS know-how. Many other OPM courses address the five workplace competencies. Job descriptions and employee evaluations and the skill centers that OPM is encouraging will have to follow suit.

SCANS know-how should also be taught in federally funded training programs for disadvantaged youth and adults, including displaced workers, under the Job Training Partnership Act (JTPA) of the Department of Labor, and public assistance training under the JOBS program of the Department of Health and Human Services.

4. **The Federal Government should continue to bridge the gap between school and the high-performance workplace, by advancing the SCANS agenda.**

In a future high-performance economy virtually all students completing school should find high-wage, high-skill jobs with advancement prospects. Children of the poor and immigrants, and women, would be full participants. In that economy, high school certification, based in part on SCANS know-how, would provide an easy and natural link between school and workplace. This economy would diminish the barriers that face those who begin life with few financial resources.

But that world and that economy do not exist today. Today only a fraction of jobs are in high-performance workplaces, and few of these are open to young people with only high school credentials. Many young people see no chance of good jobs, even if they work hard in school. Realizing the SCANS vision of linking school directly to workplace success, of using certification as a motivator for school effort, requires surmounting many obstacles.

If the bridge between school and workplace is to be constructed, the Federal Government must continue the leadership it displayed in the creation of this Commission and the related efforts of the Secretary of Labor. An example is the Commission on Work-Based Learning, whose partnership with the private sector and state and local leaders will advance standard setting and certification of employment skills. That commission currently is working to develop voluntary skill standards around core SCANS proficiencies for a number of major U.S. industries.

As the SCANS work draws to a close, the growing nationwide conversation about standard setting and assessment is impressive. In the public sector that conversation involves Federal panels, commissions, and agencies, along with state and local initiatives. In the private sector, it draws on business organizations, associations of similar firms (e.g., small manufacturers), and industry-specific groups (e.g., the hospitality industry). In the nonprofit world it benefits from the perspective of foundations, universities, think tanks, testing organizations, community-based organizations, representatives of minority populations, and academic associations concerned with specific disciplines. Labor organizations, which represent workers who feel the direct effects of standards testing and assessment activities, are actively participating. Parents also are increasingly involved. All have something to contribute; each group brings a unique piece of the puzzle to the table. This conversation is, in fact, what the United States is all about—public discussion of great public issues.

An urgent need exists for Federal leadership to bring these many efforts together. Despite the different emphases, the efforts are directed toward the same goal: establishing an equitable, nationwide system of human resource development, assessment, and certification. Whatever strengthens one, strengthens all. Working together, they can make more substantial progress toward the common end.

A partnership built around employment skills—one that includes the U.S. Departments of Labor and Education, the business community, trade unions, education, business schools, job-training and literacy providers, the military,

and community-based organizations—could accomplish a great deal. It could draw on and support the work of existing groups. It could continue the task of mapping the elements of the SCANS know-how and advance the tasks of standard setting and assessment outlined in this document. It can pursue the form that new student résumés should take, and it can encourage employers throughout the country to begin to interact with schools around these résumés, and to rely on them as a resource for creating the high-performance workplace.

A national partnership could encourage a dialogue between two major groups, one based largely in the world of work, the other consisting mostly of educators. On the one hand, we have an effort to support the development of portable certificates for specific industries by the Department of Labor's Commission on Work-Based Learning. On the other, we have the remarkable array of assessment and certification activities in the educational community: efforts to develop a national assessment system around core academic subjects, the New Standards Project (described in Chapter 6), and activities by diverse education organizations (e.g., the College Board, the Educational Testing Service, and the American College Testing program) to develop performance-based assessments of substantial portions of the SCANS know-how.

The emerging partnership can help these groups formulate their agendas and can draw on their strengths in an effort to bridge the gap between school and work. This opportunity should be seized, not squandered.

5. Every employer in America should create its own strategic vision around the principles of the high-performance workplace.

All the American high-performance success stories point in the same direction: American employers—public and private, global and local, manufacturers and innkeepers, health care providers and service organizations, whether large or small—must jettison the perspective exemplified by mottos such as, "Tell me what to do but keep it simple," and, "How long will it take, but keep it short." In the interests of long-term profitability, the Commission believes managers must restructure the workplace around the principles of high performance, continuously improving the quality of their goods and services.

The obligation for taking the first step rests with management. Experts agree that the transformation to high performance does not begin in the secretarial pool or on the plant floor. It happens because those in the executive suite and the boardroom commit themselves to achieving high quality. It is the responsibility of employers to assess their own operations against the ideal of high performance and high quality—and to follow through on the human resource implications of those principles. Thus they will take the first steps in the long journey toward the ideal that will empower workers and make them secure in their jobs.

It is simplistic to think that one formula will work for all. Each organization will have to answer the following questions for itself: What external forces and conditions are acting upon us? What do we have to do to become a high-performance organization? What does "customer satisfaction" or "total quality" mean inside this operation? What do we have to do to empower our employees so that they can help us make the transformation we need to make? The important thing is to get started, whether the effort is guided by the ideas of Edwards Deming, the MIT Commission on Industrial Productivity, the Commission on the Skills of the American Workforce, Peter Drucker, or other experts on organizational improvement.

Because of international competition, American manufacturing firms are furthest along in the transformation to high performance. But even in the manufacturing sector the high-performance workplace is more the exception than the rule. Further progress can be made as more large firms adopt the perspective of total quality management, and as more of them begin to insist that their vendors become high-performance organizations in their own right. Large firms cannot improve their own product quality if the vendors on which they rely for parts and components are not also dedicated to total quality and consumer satisfaction.

This Commission believes that dedication to quality and customer satisfaction is equally critical to market success in the service side of the economy. The nation cannot afford health and social services that leave patients or clients unhappy; restaurants, hotels, or clothing stores that permit customers to stand around ignored; transportation services characterized by delay or unreliability; or financial institutions that mishandle depositors' funds. Although the application of high-performance principles may be more difficult in the service sector than in manufacturing—and perhaps less amenable to statistical controls—the principles can be applied.[24]

A FINAL WORD

These recommendations define a comprehensive nationwide agenda. We propose it not lightly but knowing that major portions of it are already being developed, implemented, tested, and refined in hundreds of schools and businesses around the country. This document is an effort to pull the experience and wisdom of these efforts together so that local leaders can, community by community, school by school, and—if need be—classroom by classroom, begin to create their own high-performance programs.

When all is said and done, the high-performance future requires a radically different organization of work and a radically different kind of workforce. The ability of managers and workers to get the best out of new technologies, new processes, and new markets remains our best competitive advantage. Technology itself is not the answer; anyone can buy it. Wealth itself is of little help; capital is portable. More and more, success is the product of the knowledge, skills, and judgment of a valued workforce. Only that intangible quality of trained intelligence and skills actively engaged in meeting consumers' needs is nontransferable. Developing that quality will call for the best in us all.

The tasks just outlined will not be accomplished tomorrow. This Commission does not underestimate the difficulties; neither can it ignore the fact that delay will only compound them. If the nation's educators and employers move forward immediately, the agenda set forth here can be well in place by the year 2000. With it in place, the United States will have taken a major step forward toward a high-performance future and a high-wage, full-employment economy.

---

[24]Federal Express, for example, won the Baldrige Award in 1990.

---★---

PART II

A BLUEPRINT FOR
HIGH PERFORMANCE

PART II
INTRODUCTION

The SCANS effort takes place against the backdrop of an intense, nationwide self-examination about education and training, workplace needs, and the imperative for reorganizing work. Among the prominent features of this discussion are the following:

- The publication in 1987 of *Workforce 2000*, sponsored by the Department of Labor, which joined the issues of education and our economic prosperity in the year 2000;

- President Bush's education summit with the nation's governors in 1989 and their subsequent adoption in 1990 of six national education goals;

- The September 1991 "report card" on American education issued by the National Education Goals Panel;

- New education and job-training efforts from the Bush Administration, *America 2000* and *Job Training 2000,* calling for restructuring schools and improving service delivery in adult training;

- Growing consensus among many blue-ribbon groups, such as the Commission on the Skills of the American Workforce and the MIT Commission on Industrial Productivity, that the American workplace needs to be reformed around principles of high performance.

- Bush Administration and congressional efforts to encourage school improvement;

- The call of the National Council on Education Standards and Testing for a new nationwide assessment system;

- The work of the Labor Department's Commission on Work-Based Learning to develop portable certificates of employee competency industry by industry; and

- The serious debate in many states and local communities—from Rhode Island to Oregon—about how to respond to these issues.

The SCANS contribution to this national discussion includes attention to the way broad principles are to be put in place at the local level. We recognize that nationwide policies are of little value until they are advanced by men and women on the front line.

This Commission's initial publication, *What Work Requires of School*, has already begun to have an effect beyond Washington. Individual school districts in Fort Worth, Tampa, Louisville, and elsewhere are using that report in their planning processes.[25] Youngsters in Indiana, through a project called IndianaPLUS, have gone out to discover for themselves whether SCANS know-how applies in that state. And there are proposals to replicate that project in other states and cities. The Los Angeles Unified School District has announced that all its graduates, beginning in

---

[25]SCANS will publish the set of resource materials listed in Appendix C. The volume that will describe these efforts will be called *Teaching the SCANS Competencies.*

EXHIBIT E

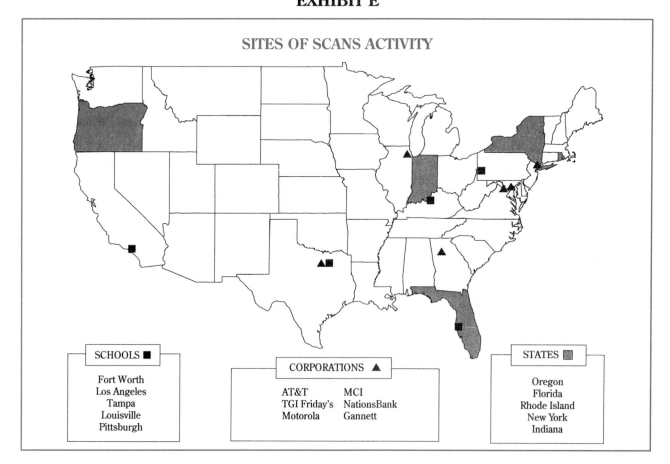

SITES OF SCANS ACTIVITY

SCHOOLS ■

Fort Worth
Los Angeles
Tampa
Louisville
Pittsburgh

CORPORATIONS ▲

AT&T   MCI
TGI Friday's NationsBank
Motorola   Gannett

STATES ▨

Oregon
Florida
Rhode Island
New York
Indiana

1994, will be warranted to have the SCANS know-how. A newly formed Human Development Corporation in the Pittsburgh area is developing a regionwide mathematics and science curriculum incorporating the SCANS workplace competencies. Florida is the first state to make the SCANS know-how an official part of its statewide educational reform program by incorporating the SCANS competencies into its student performance standards.[26] Oregon's school reform effort will include new standards based on the SCANS know-how. New York and Rhode Island are considering ways to incorporate the SCANS recommendations into new initiatives. A number of groups seeking to design "break the mold" schools are integrating SCANS know-how into their concepts. Exhibit E locates the sites of activities related to the SCANS message as of the date of this report.

In the corporate sector, TGI Friday's and Motorola are investigating ways of integrating SCANS skills into their human resource planning. In April 1992, MCI and the Gannett Corporation began to examine together the use-

---

[26]Memorandum, Florida Department of Education, March 19, 1992.

fulness of SCANS findings for the structure of job descriptions; their goal is to build the results into their educational and training activities. The Alliance for Employee Growth and Development, the training organization formed by AT&T and its major unions, has asked its vendors to determine whether they can teach the SCANS know-how. The associations that represent the hospitality and manufacturing industries are identifying how SCANS ideas can be used by their members. NationsBank, concerned about the economic well-being of the smaller communities that it serves, has begun a dialogue about teaching SCANS competencies with the Crossroads Consortium in southwestern Virginia.

The Department of Labor is moving to build SCANS workplace competency training into various aspects of its JTPA programs. The Office of Personnel Management (with the Department of Labor) is reviewing the application of SCANS ideas in skills centers for Federal employees. The Department of Defense is reviewing possible roles for SCANS training in the military and in the schools it operates overseas for military dependents.

The recommendations contained in Chapter 3 cannot be met unless these efforts are repeated throughout the worlds of education, business, and government. This second part of the SCANS final report is an effort to provide suggestions and guidance to educators, trainers, and employers about how the broad SCANS agenda can be put in place in local communities. It is organized around three major issues: reinventing education, encouraging work-based learning and high-performance industries, and restructuring assessment.

Chapter 4
SCHOOLS THAT WORK: ORGANIZING EDUCATION FOR HIGH PERFORMANCE

When the President of the United States announced the *America 2000* strategy in 1991, he called on all Americans to become revolutionaries in the cause of education. *America 2000* is an effort to reach six national education goals from four different directions: (1) reinvented schools for tomorrow's students; (2) better, more accountable schools for today's students; (3) lifelong learning for yesterday's students; and (4) supportive communities where learning for all can take place.[27] This chapter suggests how the SCANS know-how can be taught in reinvented schools where that know-how is integrated into the curriculum, teaching is done in context, and new resources provide teachers with the tools they need. The reinvention begins with a willingness to change.

COMMIT TO TRANSFORMATION

The American public school system was designed to serve the nation's economic and social needs of the turn of the century. At that time, the thinking for the workplace was done by a small portion of the population, certainly no more than a quarter of all workers. School systems, in keeping with the industrial model of the day, were highly centralized. Decisions flowed down from the top and the basic teaching method was "teacher talk"—the teacher dispensed information from the front of the classroom, while the students sat passively like buckets waiting to be filled.

During the 1980s the United States, seeking to improve public schools, tried to get more results out of that system—through tighter curricula, higher certification standards for teachers, and more testing of everyone.[28] Despite the effort, students were performing essentially no better at the end of the decade than they were at the beginning. The strategy of getting more out of the old system was doomed from the outset.

As this Commission argued in *What Work Requires of Schools*, American society today requires that elementary and secondary schools meet drastically different goals. The job now is to bring all students to a level that, in the past, only a small minority reached. Experts universally agree that this job requires reinventing elementary and secondary education.

---

[27]The six national education goals for the year 2000 adopted by the President and the nation's governors in 1990 are (1) improving readiness for school, (2) increasing high school graduation rates, (3) improving student achievement, (4) raising science and mathematics achievement, (5) improving adult literacy and skills, and (6) ridding schools of drugs and violence.

[28]Much of this discussion about education reform reflects a briefing provided to the Commission by Edward (Ted) Fiske, former education editor for the *New York Times* and author of *Smart Schools, Smart Kids* (New York: Simon and Schuster, 1991).

We recommend that SCANS know-how be taught from kindergarten through grade 12 and beyond. Even in the early grades, the foundation skills and the workplace competencies can be taught, oriented around school- and home-based tasks. As we noted in *What Work Requires of Schools*, it is not true that everything one needs to know in life is learned in kindergarten, but it is certainly true that one can begin to learn everything one needs to know that early. The five workplace competencies can be integrated with the three-part foundation as a part of every child's education from kindergarten through grade 12.

The SCANS competencies must be integrated into core academic subjects such as English and mathematics (see Exhibit F). But these skills apply across the board—to health and physical education, to music and the other arts, and to student activities normally thought to be extracurricular, such as drama and student publications. It is also important that the SCANS competencies be integrated into vocational offerings (see Sidebar A).

The process of reinvention needed to integrate SCANS know-how into the curriculum is under way across the nation. As already indicated, several local communities and organizations have started redesigning their educational offerings around the SCANS agenda. Their experience indicates that working on a SCANS-like approach only begins with curriculum and instructional reform. It often also involves redesigning the entire delivery system—introducing school-based management, shared decision making, and new means of assessment.[29]

When a school system and its surrounding community take up the SCANS agenda, what are they taking on? How difficult is the task? Who has to be involved? And what are the results likely to be? No single answer to any of these questions exists. The Commission can offer the educational community no single template for reinvention. The practical difficulties of reshaping the educational enterprise, root and branch, should not be underestimated. Nevertheless, certain conditions need to be present if the schools are to respond effectively to the SCANS message. These conditions include the following:

- Schools and communities must develop a commitment to change and a willingness to take action.

- The entire community must participate in the effort—schools, large and small businesses, community and civic leaders, labor organizations, community-based organizations, parents, the media, and state agencies (Sidebar B shows the participation throughout Indiana).

- Schools must act on the belief that improving the match between what work requires and what students are taught requires improving *how* students are taught.

- Learning must be allowed to take place in real-world contexts.

- Communities must understand that redesigning schools around skills is not simply a marginal change involving curriculum, but a basic reform strategy

---

[29]See *Teaching the SCANS Competencies* (forthcoming).

EXHIBIT F

ASSIGNMENTS THAT INTEGRATE THE SCANS COMPETENCIES INTO THE CORE CURRICULUM AREAS

Competency	English/Writing	Mathematics	Science	Social Studies/Geography	History
Resources	Write a proposal for an after-school career lecture series that schedules speakers, coordinates audio-visual aids, and estimates costs.	Develop a monthly family budget, taking into account family expenses and revenues and using information from the budget plan. Schedule a vacation trip that stays within the resources available.	Plan the material and time requirements for a chemistry experiment, to be performed over a two-day period, that demonstrates a natural growth process in terms of resource needs.	Design a chart of resource needs for a community of African Zulus. Analyze the reasons why three major cities grew to their current size.	Study the Vietnam War, researching and orally presenting findings on the timing and logistics of transporting materials and troops to Vietnam and on the impact of the war on the Federal budget.
Interpersonal	Discuss the pros and cons of the argument that Shakespeare's *Merchant of Venice* is a "racist" play and should be banned from the school curriculum.	Present the results of a survey to the class, and justify the use of specific statistics to analyze and represent the data.	Work in a group to design an experiment to analyze the lead content in the school's water. Teach the results to an elementary school class.	Debate the issue of withdrawing U.S. military support from Japan in front of a peer panel. Engage in a mock urban planning exercise for Paris.	Study the American Constitution and role-play the negotiation of the wording of the free states/slave states clause by different signers.
Information	Identify and abstract passages from a novel to support an assertion about the values of a key character.	Design and carry out a survey and analyze the data in a spreadsheet program using algebraic formulas. Develop a table and a graphic display to communicate the results.	In an entrepreneurship project, present statistical data pertaining to a high-tech company's production and sales. Use a computer to develop the statistical charts.	Using numerical data and charts, develop and present conclusions about the effects of economic conditions on the quality of life in several countries.	Research and present papers on the effect of the Industrial Revolution on the class structure in Britain, citing data sources used to arrive at conclusions.

(Continued)

EXHIBIT F
(Continued)

ASSIGNMENTS THAT INTEGRATE THE SCANS COMPETENCIES
INTO THE CORE CURRICULUM AREAS

Competency	English/Writing	Mathematics	Science	Social Studies/Geography	History
Systems	Develop a computer model that analyzes the motivation of Shakespeare's *Hamlet*. Plot the events that increase or decrease Hamlet's motivation to avenge the death of his father.	Develop a system to monitor and correct the heating/cooling process in a computer laboratory, using principles of statistical process control.	Build a model of human population growth that includes the impact of the amount of food available, on birth and death rates, etc. Do the same for a growth model for insects.	Analyze the accumulation of capital in industrialized nations in systems terms (as a reinforcing process with stocks and flows).	Develop a model of the social forces that led to the American Revolution. Then explore the fit between that model and other revolutions.
Technology	Write an article showing the relationship between technology and the environment. Use word processing to write and edit papers after receiving teacher feedback.	Read manuals for several data-processing programs and write a memo recommending the best programs to handle a series of mathematical situations.	Calibrate a scale to weigh accurate portions of chemicals for an experiment. Trace the development of this technology from earliest uses to today.	Research and report on the development and functions of the seismograph and its role in earthquake prediction and detection.	Analyze the effects of wars on technological development. Use computer graphics to plot the relationship of the country's economic growth to periods of peace and war.

36

INTEGRATING SCANS KNOW-HOW INTO ARTS AND VOCATIONAL-TECHNICAL EDUCATION

The Arts and High Performance

SCANS know-how can be learned in the context of the arts. At a pragmatic level, high school students learning to make charts could benefit from knowing more about the visual arts. The advent of desktop publishing means that millions of workers will be publishing documents, deciding how to make them visually appealing, and, in general, calling on talents that only yesterday were primarily the concern of graphic artists.

The theater arts are often thought of as developing speaking, reading, and listening skills. But theater people also know about another domain of the SCANS know-how, **managing the resources** of time, money, space, and people. Participation in school performances teaches students about schedules, budgets, space layout, staffing, and the **interpersonal skills,** such as teaching others and working as a team. **Technology** use is another of the SCANS competencies. Musical instruments are becoming increasingly high-tech. Some synthesized sounds come directly from sophisticated mathematical functions fed into a musical instrument digital interface. **Systems,** the fifth SCANS competency, can be taught in the context of orchestral composition.

Arts education naturally embraces methods that are characteristic of high-performance schools. Art departments often accept and evaluate students on the basis of portfolios and auditioned performances. Coaching and assessing progress are done continuously in the midst of practice, performance, or critiques. The arts are an especially good vehicle for teaching about improving quality. Who, more than the artist, is unwilling to be satisfied with yesterday's performance?

Vocational-Technical Education and Workplace Know-How

Few educators are more aware of the importance of teaching workplace know-how than those in vocational-technical education. Vocational education can shape itself into high-performance centers for training by incorporating the SCANS foundation skills into its curriculum. Reading, writing, math, and science are currently being woven into vocational studies to enhance the ability of students to achieve the SCANS workplace competencies.

Recognizing the need to teach basic academic, thinking, and interpersonal skills, vocational education is also progressively becoming a team-teaching effort. Academic and vocational teachers work side by side to reinforce the relevance of academics by demonstrating how they apply to the high-performance workplace.

This restructuring empowers students to use the information they are given to evaluate and organize data and apply it to solve problems. When students understand the job that needs to be done, allocating resources of time, money, materials, personnel, and information is learned in the context of application. Vocational-technical education answers the question often asked by students ("Why should I learn this?") by demonstrating how the productive use of resources, interpersonal skills, information, systems, and technology is necessary to achieve excellence in business and industry. Because the link between school and work becomes clear, school takes on new relevance.

affecting management, instruction, and assessment.

- Educators must rethink assessment so that it is compatible with the instructional strategies chosen to deliver the SCANS know-how, and reinforces, guides, and motivates instruction and learning.

In this regard, the Commission supports the nine points of the education-reform program developed by the Business Roundtable, an association of the chief executive officers of many of our nation's largest employers.[30]

The Fort Worth Experience[31]

The reinvention experience in Fort Worth, Texas, provides a case study of the degree of change required. The Fort Worth Independent School District is in the front ranks of the effort to restructure American public education in two respects: Fort Worth business, civic, and educational leaders have a vision of where they are going, and they understand that the time for tinkering with the existing system is over. They also understand that genuine improvement can be created only if everyone with a stake in the outcome—parents, students, administrators, teachers, and business leaders—is involved.

The Fort Worth Metropolitan Area, with a population exceeding 1.3 million, is home to several major corporate headquarters, many manufacturing and distribution facilities, and some 700 high-technology companies. The district enrolls an ethnically and culturally diverse student population of about 68,000 (35 percent African American, 26 percent Hispanic), housed in 110 schools and taught by 3,500 teachers.

The idea of getting business and civic groups involved with the schools was discussed with the Board of Education and then taken to the Fort Worth Chamber of Commerce. The result was Project C³—Community, Corporations, Classrooms—an effort to create an educational system that motivates and prepares students for success in school, in the workplace, as citizens, and in their personal lives.

The first step in Fort Worth was similar to the first step in the work of this Commission: find out what skills and competencies the workplace demands. Fort Worth's leaders decided that the logical place to start was by asking people in the local workplace themselves—the employers (nearly 300) and employees (nearly 3,000). The Fort Worth investigation confirmed

---

[30]*Essential Components of a Successful Education System,* (New York.: Business Roundtable, n.d.). The nine points are these: (1) The new system is committed to four operating assumptions: (a) All students can learn at significantly higher levels. (b) We know how to teach all students successfully. (c) Curriculum content must reflect high expectations for all students, but instructional time and strategies may vary to assure success. (d) Every child must have an advocate. (2) The new system is based on performance or outcomes. (3) Assessment strategies must be as strong and rich as the outcomes. (4) Schools should receive rewards for success and assistance to improve. (5) School-based staff have a major role in making instructional decisions. (6) Major emphasis is placed on staff development. (7) A high-quality prekindergarten program is established, at least for all disadvantaged students. (8) Health and other social services are sufficient to reduce significant barriers to learning. (9) Technology is used to raise student and teacher productivity and to expand access to learning.

[31]This section and the next one draw extensively from a review of the Fort Worth, Texas, experience with restructuring schooling as reported in Michael Kane et al., *Developing Schools That Work* (Fort Worth: Fort Worth Public Schools, 1992).

the importance of reading, mathematics, writing, speaking and listening, computer literacy, reasoning and problem solving, and originality and creativity.

The second step Fort Worth took was to develop educational programming that is responsive to workplace needs. To date, the school district has several efforts under way:

Applied Learning relates learning more directly to the needs of the workplace. The project involves 38 teachers in some 24 schools who have created instructional models to develop the skills identified in the C³ project and by SCANS.

Vital Link bridges the gap between school and business. Sponsored nationally by the American Business Conference, this initiative is being carried out by the Fort Worth Chamber of Commerce which has 3,800 members. It lets both students and teachers experience what work requires through teacher and student internships.

Equity 2000, sponsored by The College Board, upgrades mathematics instruction—and hence skills in reasoning and thinking—by dropping less rigorous mathematics offerings and requiring all students to progress through a demanding sequence including algebra and geometry. The initial results are impressive: among Hispanics, 75 per-

SIDEBAR B

IndianaPLUS: MODEL "SCHOOL TO WORK " PROJECT

Based on the SCANS findings and methods and the initiative of the American Broadcasting Company (ABC), teams of high school seniors in five Indiana cities systematically explored the world of work during the first semester of the 1991-92 school year. This pilot project, known as "IndianaPLUS," is described in *Teaching the SCANS Competencies* (see Appendix C). Efforts are under way to help other states and communities that wish to mount similar projects.

Each team of 20 to 25 students worked under the supervision of a social studies teacher at high schools in Evansville, Fort Wayne, Indianapolis, South Bend, and Terre Haute. Aided by local Junior Achievement offices, ABC-affiliated television stations, and business leaders, the students interviewed a range of job-holders to pinpoint the skills required in the local economy. Each student interviewed three to five workers, using a modified version of the SCANS interview method.

Based on the interviews and other research, each team produced videotapes and handbooks to help communicate to middle-school students what the team had learned about workforce needs. The local television stations spread the message to the general public. (ABC affiliates were involved as part of the network's Project Literacy United States–PLUS.)

The culmination of the project came with the televising of a special hour-long program on the skills gap in Indiana and on the work of the "IndianaPLUS" teams. Aired in prime time simultaneously by all five television affiliates, the statewide special was hosted by Peter Jennings of ABC News and by local news anchors in the five cities. It presented the issues of global competition, technological change, and the skills gap, and then focused on the local findings of the IndianaPLUS students and teachers.

cent more males and 43 percent more females enrolled in algebra in the 1991-92 school year; among African-American students, 33 percent more males and 41 percent more females enrolled.

Vocational education has been substantially modified, with the help of school-based advisory committees, to gear the curriculum more closely to local work requirements. One result has been the districtwide adoption of a new Principles of Technology course that embeds advanced mathematical and scientific principles in the study of electronics, hydraulics, and mechanics.

High-Performance Schools, a joint venture between district and business leaders, brings the principles of site-based management and decision making to Fort Worth schools. This project includes districtwide training for principals, administrators, and school teams and a school incentive grant program.

Student Assessment is in the process of being transformed on the theory that multiple-choice, paper-and-pencil tests cannot evaluate students' ability to apply knowledge to real-world problems. The Portfolio Project is developing portfolios of student competencies that include a personal résumé, evidence of competence in specific areas of study, work history, extracurricular experience, and record of community services. This effort is connected to the New Standards Project, discussed in Chapter 6.

Despite all these initiatives, Fort Worth recognizes it has just begun the process of fully restructuring its schools. The city's education and business leaders, represented by the local Chamber of Commerce, are moving to transform the system in accordance with the lessons these initiatives provide.

THE INSTRUCTIONAL STRATEGY: TEACH IN CONTEXT

In its 1991 report, this Commission argued that learning in order "to know" should not be separated from learning in order "to do." We concluded that the two could be combined by teaching "in context," that is, learning content while solving realistic problems. Teaching in context implies that students and teachers will learn and apply knowledge in real-life situations, for example, by participating in work-based projects, internships, and mentor programs and by "shadowing" workers on the job. IndianaPLUS is a work-based project, and the Fort Worth experiment offers students and teachers all these activities.

Another of the promising "applied academics" developments being implemented in Fort Worth and by high schools and community colleges across the nation is the 2+2 tech-prep/associate degree program, which could easily incorporate the SCANS know-how. In one community this program, now funded with Federal funds through the Carl D. Perkins Vocational Education and Applied Technology Act, "had the greatest impact on secondary education since high school consolidation in 1971. Since beginning the tech-prep program, average SAT scores have increased 46 points, the dropout rate has declined significantly, and the percentage of graduates choosing to attend a community college rose from 24 to 46 percent!"[32]

Teaching in context is different from making up artificial word problems (e.g., the classic algebra problem that requires students to determine when two trains leaving different stations at the same time will meet). For example, chemistry students in Fort Worth learned how chemistry applies to the problem of growing grass on the grounds at 104 Fort Worth schools. They then presented the results of their work to the school board for policy action.

Teaching in context requires more complex integration with real-world experience. It also often requires cooperative learning opportunities (e.g., peer teaching and group problem solving). It always demands that students be active learners—that is, *workers*—who are promoting the growth of their own knowledge as they undertake realistic tasks. And it requires that the curriculum be integrated across subject areas in activities that require students to read, write, compute, apply scientific or statistical principles, integrate, and reason about specific problems.

Exhibit G, drawn from experience in Fort Worth, outlines how the conventional classroom differs from the SCANS classroom. The conventions of today's classroom (teacher omniscience, student passivity and isolation, rigid disciplinary borders, and "abstracted" knowledge and facts) are replaced with sophisticated and more realistic concepts of instruction and learning (the teacher may not know best, students often learn best in groups, and knowledge should be related to real problems).

Wishful thinking will not create such classrooms. Fort Worth found that these classrooms require community support, parental leadership, business support, and site-based management that allows individual schools to get out from under the dead hand of regulation. The school system is making a searching examination of instructional strategies to make sure that "in context" learning is encouraged around the SCANS workplace competencies. Systemic change will require appropriate instructional materials and technology for delivering the SCANS know-how and the resources, including training and time, that teachers and administrators need to do the job right.

What does it mean to organize instructional strategies around in-context learning? How did Fort Worth change its instructional strategy?

One of the district's first projects was to examine the way writing is taught. Good writing could be taught in virtually every subject: English, social studies, foreign languages, vocational programs, and even mathematics and the sciences. In English, where literature and poetry are discussed, writing and reading are related to aesthetic experience and the role of education is self-realization. Writing in history is often related to the educational goal of enhancing citizenship.

In mathematics and the physical or social sciences, however, writing may be ignored or treated in the same way as writing for an aesthetic experience. As a result, graduates often cannot write a memo. How should the

---

[32]School Superintendent Douglas James of Richmond County, North Carolina. The 2+2 tech-prep/associate degree program was first advocated by SCANS Commissioner Dale Parnell in his book *The Neglected Majority*, published by the American Association of Community and Junior Colleges in 1985.

EXHIBIT G

THE CONVENTIONAL CLASSROOM COMPARED WITH THE SCANS CLASSROOM	
FROM THE CONVENTIONAL CLASSROOM	**TO THE SCANS CLASSROOM**
Teacher knows answer.	More than one solution may be viable and teacher may not have it in advance.
Students routinely work alone.	Students routinely work with teachers, peers, and community members.
Teacher plans all activities.	Students and teachers plan and negotiate activities.
Teacher makes all assessments. Information is organized, evaluated, interpreted and communicated to students by teacher.	Students routinely assess themselves. Information is acquired, evaluated, organized, interpreted, and communicated by students to appropriate audiences.
Organizing system of the classroom is simple: one teacher teaches 30 students.	Organizing systems are complex: teacher and students both reach out beyond school for additional information.
Reading, writing, and math are treated as separate disciplines; listening and speaking often are missing from curriculum.	Disciplines needed for problem solving are integrated; listening and speaking are fundamental parts of learning.
Thinking is usually theoretical and "academic."	Thinking involves problem solving, reasoning, and decision making.
Students are expected to conform to teacher's behavioral expectations; integrity and honesty are monitored by teacher; students' self-esteem is often poor. Source: Fort Worth Public Schools.	Students are expected to be responsible, sociable, self-managing, and resourceful; integrity and honesty are monitored within the social context of the classroom; students' self-esteem is high because they are in charge of own learning.

teaching of writing be refocused? Some writing assignments should be reoriented from the academic focus preferred in today's school to the kinds of writing demands found in the real world of work. Most decent jobs today require some level of writing ability. For some professionals, writing is the only thing they do. For others, at all levels in the organization, writing is an intermittent obligation to develop letters, memoranda, reports, or presentations that range from relatively easy and rewarding to relatively difficult and unpleasant.

Exhibit H compares the writing that today's schools teach and what the workplace requires. The contrast is dramatic. The school sees writing as an academic exercise—essays, book reports, research papers—designed to demonstrate mastery of academic knowledge, skills, content, and format. The audience is limited to one person (the teacher), and the novice writer is obliged to tell everything he or she has discovered. The logic is conceptual and theoretical, but at the same time neatness, punctuation, and grammar may be the main basis for evaluation.

EXHIBIT H

WRITING: THE SCANS PERSPECTIVE

What Today's Schools Teach	What the Workplace Requires
Purposes for Writing	
• Central purpose is to display mastery of knowlege, skills, and format.	• Range of purposes (instrumental): to inform, persuade, clarify (or obscure), soften the blow, explain how to do something, tell others to do something, make a recommendation, sell.
Types of Writing Routinely Generated	
• Essays, book reports, poetry, stories, research papers, letters.	• Reports, brochures, letters, memos, proposals, surveys, ad copy, instructions, planning documents, messages, specifications, recommendations, logs, legal documents/contracts, news releases, minutes, personnel evaluations.
Audience	
• Single audience: the teacher.	• A range of audiences, including people differing in needs, motivations, uses for the information, and knowledge of the topic, e.g., supervisors, clients, co-workers, subordinates, the general public.
Work Conditions	
• Deadlines and distractions controlled by the teacher.	• Deadlines and distractions often unavoidable.
Content	
• Teacher assigns topics. • Text reveals everything discovered.	• Ill-defined problems are worked through. • Text tells what the reader needs to know.
Logic	
• Theoretical; "academic."	• Problem-solving, pragmatic, goal-oriented.
Correctness	
• Usage, handwriting, spelling, and punctuation are a focus for evaluation, accounting for 50 to 100 percent of the document's value.	• Same factors are a given, not a focus for evaluation.

Source: Fort Worth Public Schools.

In contrast, workplace writing is always developed for a purpose—often to explain or to persuade a group to act on a recommendation. The documents usually have a variety of audiences, and the writer's obligation is to tell the readers something they do not know but need to know. Far from working on well-defined topics selected by the teacher, the working writer has to cope with poorly defined problems amid the distractions of other demands and tight deadlines. Both kinds of writing require neatness and good grammar, but in the workplace these factors are just the beginning, not the goal.

ADDITIONAL RESOURCES

Education will have to invest in change. By investment we mean expenditures whose effect will be felt for years to come. Among the most important investments are staff development, technology, and instructional materials. All should increase the quality produced by the workers in the system: the teachers and their students.

Training and Time

Of all the resources required for reinventing schools around the SCANS ends, none is more important than those devoted to staff development and teacher training. Teachers, noninstructional staff, and building and school-district administrators will need extensive assistance in developing the following:

- *New pedagogical skills* required to teach in context and to develop active, collaborative, learning environments;

- *New instructional management skills* needed to use the instructional technologies to find new ways of interacting with students; and

- *Knowledge and understanding of the principles of high performance* as they are applied in restructured workplaces.

Providing training opportunities for instructional staff in these areas will be costly. Perhaps the major expense will involve giving teachers and administrators the time they need during the school day and summers to work on these activities.[33]

Technology

A 1990 study from the Congressional Office of Technology Assessment[34] pointed out that, in its operations and purposes, education is very much like the information industry in the private sector. But unlike other information industries (banking, finance, and insurance, for example) which have been remade by technolo-

---

[33]If a school devotes $300 per student for teacher training and development activities in its annual budget (about 5 percent of the current cost per student), and the student-teacher ratio is 25:1, each teacher would have $7,500 to use for training. This money could be used in a number of ways, such as:

- Paying for 250 hours of training at $30 per hour (perhaps in a business environment) during the summer; or

- Enabling a group of teachers to pool their training resources so that the school could hire an additional staff member. The new staff member would substitute for each member of the group one day a month while group members participate in training.

[34]Office of Technology Assessment, *Power On! New Tools for Teaching and Learning* (Washington, D.C.: U.S. Government Printing Office, September 1988).

gy and its applications, the information-technology revolution of the last generation has had little effect in education. The basic technology available to most teachers throughout the United States in 1992 is too close to the technology of 1892: textbooks, blackboards, and chalk.

Yet technologies offering the promise of revolutionizing teaching and learning are readily available. CD/ROM (compact disk/read only memory) players, personal computers, and integrated learning systems are currently being used effectively in a number of schools across the country. The new CD-I (compact disk interactive) technology and broadcast-based interactive video will be on the consumer market this year. These technologies are capable of providing multiple learning contexts and resources for students in cost-effective ways: delivering self-paced instruction, monitoring and continuously assessing learning, and placing students in real-life and real-work simulations with multimedia presentations.

Even more promising are instructional tools that allow students to use the same technology that adults use at work. For example, word processing makes it easier for students to submit multiple drafts of a paper. In short, technology offers the opportunity to change the roles that teachers and students have traditionally played. With technology dispensing information, teachers are free to coach and facilitate student learning. With technology monitoring learning, students can become active learners, working to effectively acquire new skills as they solve problems. If the goal of creating high-performance learning organizations is to be realized, the reinvention of American education has to incorporate these new tools.[35]

Instructional Materials

The SCANS workplace competencies will not be widely taught unless teachers have access to instructional materials that put them in context. These materials include textbooks, computer-based materials, and multimedia materials that employ the technology noted in the previous section. Video and multimedia materials are essential to creating the realistic contexts in which the competencies are used.

Materials are needed for the teachers of mathematics, science, English, history, and geography who will teach the SCANS competencies as part of their regular courses. A similar need exists for teachers of art, foreign language, English as a Second Language (ESL), and vocational courses. Finally, "second chance," proprietary schools, and community colleges need instructional materials for their curricula.

High-quality materials are expensive to develop. The investment—whether made by the

---

[35]To get some sense of the budgetary implications of using technology, SCANS surveyed a number of high school technology directors and technology vendors across the country. We asked them what kinds of technology they thought a school could buy with a budget allocation of $1,000 per student (which could be spread over a number of years). A high school of 1,400 students would have $1.4 million that could be devoted to acquiring technology (assuming that funds for staff training, software, and support were available separately). According to the results of our survey, most schools would purchase similar systems, including the types of technology mentioned in this paragraph. See *Teaching the SCANS Competencies* (forthcoming) for a more extensive discussion of these technologies.

public or private sector—can be justified only if many students use the materials over a period of years. If SCANS is widely adopted—and millions of students learn these skills—that condition of widespread use will be met.

Private-sector publishers will need some assurance that a market exists before making that investment. This assurance can come from a variety of sources: large-scale purchases of materials for federally financed programs, inclusion of the SCANS know-how in state curriculum frameworks, or development of joint ventures between one or more states and publish-ers (for example, Florida is developing a multimedia ESL program and another youth-at-risk program in partnership with two different publishers).

Instructional materials is one of the "chicken and egg" problems that will have to be solved if the SCANS agenda is to be realized. If publishers refrain from investing in materials development until curriculum frameworks are changed, and states refrain from changing their frameworks until instructional materials are available, no progress will be made.

Chapter 5
WORK- BASED LEARNING AND HIGH-PERFORMANCE INDUSTRIES

This Commission has said to employers, "Change your view of your human resource responsibilities. . . . Your new responsibilities must include developing the human resources in your community, your firm, and your nation." We defined a generic set of workplace competencies. If the SCANS goals are to be met, employers will have to use the language built around the SCANS know-how in all their human resource activities. They will have to teach the SCANS competencies in expanded internal training programs. The SCANS language will also have to be adopted as the definition of workplace literacy and employment preparation in second-chance programs. Finally, and most important, industry will have to build high-performance workplaces where the competencies are used and rewarded.

A COMMON LANGUAGE

Employers must become an active force in communicating what is required for success on the job. In *What Work Requires of Schools,* we created a new vocabulary for communicating the fundamental skills and competencies required by work. This vocabulary must take hold throughout the workplace. As pointed out earlier, about 80 percent of the workers on whom the American economy will depend as it enters the 21st century are already on the job. Some of these people are youngsters and young adults from age 16 to 25, who today are lost in the transition between school and work. Their high schools talked of English and geometry, but their employers speak a different language. Their frustration could be lessened by an adequate referral system that mediates between the two worlds. A system like this requires that schools and employers learn and use a common language, such as one built around the SCANS know-how.

In a workable referral system:

- Employers would describe job requirements in terms of the SCANS competencies.

- Education providers—vocational schools, proprietary schools,— in community colleges, adult education, and work-based programs—would offer instruction and certification in SCANS know-how.

- Referral agencies—job counselors in high schools, in employment agencies, and the Employment Service, or in the skill centers newly recommended by the Bush Administration—would assess their clients' SCANS know-how, understand job and educational requirements and opportunities in the same terms, and refer clients to career-enhancing work and education.

If high-performance workplaces are to become the norm rather than the exception in the American economy, promoting the SCANS know-how in the existing workforce must be widely adopted. Programs must be designed to serve adult learners, who differ from those in high school in several important ways:

- **Experience:** Adults know more and have more opinions than young people.

- **Motivation:** Adults often are not required to attend school, as are most young people.

- **Other Demands on Time:** The great demands on adults' time, the difficulties they face in traveling to "school" and adhering to a school schedule, and the objectives they bring to their learning are likely to present challenges. Most important, they need to earn a living and often cannot afford to be full-time students.

- **Financing:** Workers' education may be paid for by their companies on a voluntary basis (e.g., tuition-reimbursement schemes) or as a result of union-based negotiations (e.g., the arrangements negotiated by the United Auto Workers with the "Big Three" automobile companies). Continuing education may also be self-financed.

- **Providers:** However financed, the education may be provided by company training programs, joint union-management programs, vocational-technical schools, community colleges or four-year institutions, community-based organizations, correspondence courses, and, as technology progresses, distance-learning methods.

Adult learners, unlike younger students, are more likely to want to learn their SCANS know-how in the course of industry-specific training, rather than in traditional academic courses. Moreover, these students may be aiming for a specific profile of skills fitted to a certain job possibility or career.

In addition to their joblessness, unemployed adults experience all of the difficulties that employed adults experience. But the unemployed may be particularly eager to acquire the skills needed to find a job. Moreover, unemployed workers may be able to finance their education through publicly supported adult job-training efforts, although these workers face uncertain post training job prospects.

WORK-BASED LEARNING

For most employees, employer-sponsored education and training programs need to be created. Although the private sector spends $50 billion on education and training, precious little formal training is now being provided to front-line workers as opposed to managers. According to the Commission on the Skills of the American Workforce (CSAW), for example, only 8 percent of today's front-line employees receive any formal training on the job,[36] and this training is largely limited to orientation for new employees or short courses in such areas as safety and environmental regulation.

The CSAW findings confirm an earlier Rand Corporation study, thought to be the most comprehensive analysis of private-sector training.[37] According to the Rand analysis, about

---

[36]See NCEE, *America's Choice.* Front-line workers are those who work at the point of production or the point of sale.

[37]Lee A. Lillard and Hong W. Tan, *Private Sector Training in the United States: Who Gets It and What Are Its Effects?* (Santa Monica, Calif.: Rand Corporation, 1986).

7 percent of men receive company training in their first year of employment and 10 percent in the second year. Among women, the figures are 3.6 and 3.2 percent. Although the likelihood of receiving training increases the longer the worker remains with the same firm, training is disproportionately provided to those who need it least, that is, college graduates and those with a year or more in college. High school graduates and dropouts are at the end of the training line.

What these findings mean is displayed graphically in Exhibit I. The 25 percent of high school graduates who receive baccalaureate degrees—for example, technical professionals—are two to three times as likely to receive formal company-based training as are laborers; machine operators; and transportation, service, and clerical workers.

Measured against international standards, most American front-line workers have few training opportunities.[38] Exhibit J compares these efforts in the United States with those of three major economic competitors in terms of school-to-work transition and availability and quality of vocational education, and employer-sponsored training. The results are troubling: in the United States, the transition from school to work is left mostly to chance; vocational education is uneven; and workplace training is largely limited to managers, executives, and those already technically trained.

Islands of Excellence

There are islands of excellence in a number of corporations across the industrial spectrum (see Sidebar C). Despite the fact that many companies have recently announced major job reductions, almost all of them have in place, and plan to keep in place, companywide efforts to upgrade the skills of their workforce.

Some corporate training programs are the result of a realization by union leaders and executives of the need to make workers part of a high-performance industry. Ford and its branch of the United Auto Workers (UAW) pioneered the concept in the auto industry, and the UAW made training of front-line workers part of industrywide bargaining. Initially, five cents was contributed to a training fund for each hour worked by a UAW member (the so-called nickel fund). In recent years the contribution has risen to 10 cents per hour, or more in some circumstances.

The Communications Workers of America (CWA) brought the concept to the communications industry. When AT&T lost its regulated monopoly position, its workers also lost job security. The 1986 collective bargaining agreement between AT&T, CWA, and the International Brotherhood of Electrical Workers (IBEW) established the Alliance for Employee Growth and Development as a separate organization, with a board of directors chosen from

---

[38]OTA, *Worker Training.*

both the company and its unions. Each month, AT&T contributes to the Alliance about $13 per worker. The contribution supports the activities of 300 local union-management committees. Since its inception, more than 65,000 unionized employees have enrolled in 145,000 training activities, ranging from basic skills to advanced technology. The Alliance, working with AT&T's Business Units as they develop strategic plans, qualifies workers for the new jobs created by

EXHIBIT I

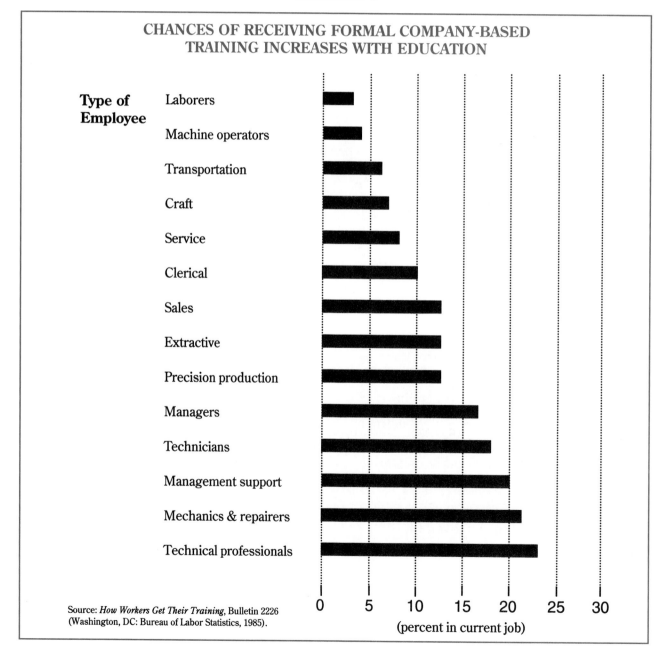

CHANCES OF RECEIVING FORMAL COMPANY-BASED TRAINING INCREASES WITH EDUCATION

Type of Employee

- Laborers
- Machine operators
- Transportation
- Craft
- Service
- Clerical
- Sales
- Extractive
- Precision production
- Managers
- Technicians
- Management support
- Mechanics & repairers
- Technical professionals

(percent in current job)

Source: *How Workers Get Their Training*, Bulletin 2226 (Washington, DC: Bureau of Labor Statistics, 1985).

50

EXHIBIT J

INTERNATIONAL COMPARISON OF WORKER TRAINING				
	United States	**Germany**	**Japan**	**Korea**
School-to-Work Transition	Left mostly to chance; some employers have ties with local schools	Apprenticeships available for most non-college-bound youth	Personal relationships cultivated between employers and local schools	Employers recruit from vocational and academic high schools
Vocational Education: Extent	Available in most areas	Universally available	Limited; mostly assumed by employers	Universally available
Quality	Wide range: poor to excellent	Uniformly good	Fair to good	Vocational high schools uniformly good
Employer-Provided Training Extent	Largely limited to managers and technicians	Widespread at entry level and needed to qualify for promotion	Widespread	Limited; employers rely on public vocational institutes
Quality	Wide range; some programs are excellent, but more are weak or unstructured	Very good	Very good	Generally poor
Public Policies	Federal role is very limited; state aid to employers is growing	Government apprenticeships encourage continuing training	Subsidies encourage training by small firms	Directive—some employers resist policies

Source: OTA, *Worker Trainin,*

changing technologies and markets. Vendors that sell training materials and services to the Alliance have been asked to describe how they could help teach the SCANS know-how.

A dramatic example of the fruits of joint union-management efforts to integrate work around quality and high performance is found in New United Motor Manufacturing, Inc.

SIDEBAR C

FROM SMALL MANUFACTURERS TO ELECTRONICS GIANTS

Across the industrial spectrum, from manufacturing to high technology, many American corporations have responded to the imperative to develop their workers. Will-Burt, Inc., and Motorola are examples.

Will-Burt, Inc. Harry Featherstone is the president and CEO of Will-Burt, Inc., a small ($20 million in sales) manufacturer located in Orrville, Ohio. Pressed by the threat of bankruptcy, a 35 percent product-rejection rate, 2,000 hours of rework per month, and a largely uneducated workforce, Featherstone has become a firm believer in and practitioner of the Deming principles. When he started, he "couldn't get 10 people to volunteer to take courses in basic blueprint reading" on company time. Now, 25 percent of the factory workers take classes on everything from accounting to inventory control, and on their own time. At the same time, product rejections fell to 8 percent and rework to 400 hours. Quality improved to the extent that Will-Burt became the first American manufacturer of gears for Honda's Gold-Wing motorcycle factory in Marysville, Ohio.

Featherstone is also a champion of a proposed Associate Degree of Manufacturing. At present he is working on the idea with the University of Akron. The degree will be (1) obtained through instruction provided by community colleges *and* employers, (2) based on the SCANS competencies as they apply to manufacturing, and (3) honored throughout the manufacturing industry because it will be backed by an industrywide organization.

Motorola Corporation, as mentioned earlier, has set itself the objective of reducing its defects to 3.4 per million components in 1992. The company has established the following education and training objectives:

- By the end of 1992, all employees worldwide will receive five days of job-relevant training and education per year.

- By the end of 1994, all employees will have mastered and applied the job skills required by business plans.

- By the end of 1995, all employees will be competent in the language, reading, and mathematics skills needed for their jobs and for higher-level training.

- By the end of 1994, all components of the program will meet criteria for high performance—best-in-class training and customer satisfaction.

- By 2000, exit-level proficiencies of the graduates of targeted institutions will be equal to or higher than entry-level skill requirements of Motorola.

(NUMMI), a joint General Motors–Toyota venture located at a former General Motors (GM) manufacturing facility in Fremont, California. Union and management committed themselves to new labor-management relationships: to resolve problems through consensus; to seek constant improvement in quality, productivity, and cost; and to resolve any worker's failure to meet work rates. The workers' right to stop the production line when quality is at risk, without fear of being disciplined, was made explicit. Finally, management agreed to reduce its own salaries and to bring work that had been contracted out back to the plant before resorting to layoffs.

NUMMI's success since opening in 1984 is impressive, particularly against the backdrop of prior experience at the same facility. An entirely new approach to management—replacing "Taylorism" with total quality management—was essential.

Other employers have similar stories to tell. Working with its union, the Xerox Corporation also annually spends millions of dollars training its employees.[39] Xerox's International Center for Training and Management Development in Virginia offers programs in sales training, service and technical courses, and management development. All told, Xerox trains 110,000 employees annually. Arthur Andersen & Company employs about 200 trainers at its Worldwide Center for Professional Education in Illinois, which last year provided training to 58,000 of the firm's employees.

Unfortunately, there is a general lack of coherence and coordination among programs offered by different employers—be they private companies or various governments. There are few portable certificates—outside the general equivalency diploma (GED) or college degrees—that many workers believe are worthwhile. Few firms recognize certificates granted by other companies' internal training programs. As a result, tuition-referral programs are undersubscribed. Employers and workers would benefit if job descriptions, career ladders, recruiting, training, and portable certificates were tied to a common language such as SCANS. The enhanced benefit would encourage employers to invest their money, and employees to invest their time in education and training.

SECOND-CHANCE PROGRAMS

Providing everyone with a "second chance" is a deeply held value in the United States. People who drop out of high school are encouraged to return or are offered the opportunity to obtain the GED. Community, technical, and junior colleges across the nation are now providing millions of adults with second-chance opportunities. Many learn skills missed in formal schooling in their military service. Unemployed people and those on public assistance can take advantage of employment-training opportunities supported by Federal and state agencies.

Since the early 1980s the principal vehicle for Federal involvement in employment and training has been the Job Training Partnership Act (JTPA). JTPA gives states and their local agents, usually private industry councils (PICs), considerable discretion in designing programs to meet local needs. Most of the services are provided not directly by the PICs themselves, but under contract with local education agencies, community colleges, proprietary schools,

---

[39]Carol Kleiman, "Recession or Not, Training Remains an Essential Expense," *Washington Post*, (January 19, 1992.)

and community-based organizations. Title II of the legislation offers employment and training services to disadvantaged persons. Title III of the legislation provides education and training services to workers dislocated by economic or technological change. Unlike the other JTPA programs, eligibility for Title III is based not on income, but the loss (or prospect of the loss) of a job.

Several other programs provide other significant Federal support for upgrading employment skills. The Carl D. Perkins Vocational Education and Applied Technology Act helps schools, community colleges, and vocational and technical institutes provide students with marketable job skills. States match $1.1 billion of Federal funds in vocational education by a factor of 10 for every Federal dollar. The Adult Education Act is oriented largely to improving functional literacy. Appropriations for Adult Education, which serves about 3.6 million adults each year, approach $300 million annually. The Job Opportunities and Basic Skills (JOBS) Training Program authorized by the Family Support Act of 1988 helps eligible welfare recipients become self-sufficient by providing education and training and other related support. Significant Federal matching funds are available for the JOBS program on an entitlement basis.

"Second chance" programs can readily be adapted to the SCANS know-how. Embedding these competencies and the foundation skills in JTPA, JOBS, vocational education, and adult education programs will make them more useful to participants and increase the return on the public's investment.

APPRENTICESHIP PROGRAMS

Apprenticeship is an age-old system of providing learning in context. Apprentices are employed in virtually every sector of the American economy, from agriculture to government. The 819 occupations recognized for apprenticeship training range, alphabetically, from accordion maker to x-ray equipment tester. The overwhelming majority of apprentices, however, are in the construction industry; 10 occupations (e.g., electrician, carpenter, plumber, machinist, tool-and-die maker) account for more than 132,000 apprentices—about 50 percent of the total.

From the SCANS perspective, the attractiveness of apprenticelike training lies in the structure of apprenticeship itself. Apprentices have to meet occupational and industry standards. They earn a living while they are learning. They receive structured, on-the-job training and related theoretical instruction. The apprentice understands how long the training will last-as little as one year to as long as five, depending on the occupation. A wage-progression schedule is normally associated with apprenticeship, and apprentices are aware of the financial benefits of completing training and of receiving their journeyman's certificate. In short, the apprenticeship model incorporates many of the elements required to teach the SCANS know-how.

TRAINING AND THE HIGH-PERFORMANCE INDUSTRY

There is a growing consensus that the productivity, stability, and competitiveness of today's firm is more and more directly tied to the quality of its workforce. Deming's emphasis on training has already been mentioned, and training is one of the six points identified as essential to manufacturing competitiveness by the MIT Commission on Industrial Productivity in 1989. Another point made both by Deming and MIT is each firm's dependence on receiving high-quality input from its suppliers. Thus, firms such as Motorola, Boeing, and Xerox require that their suppliers train to become high-performance firms.

In short, high-performance, competitive firms cannot be created or thrive if their suppliers lack the kinds of competencies and skills defined by the Commission. This is as true for service and public-sector organizations as it is for manufacturing enterprises. Good training pays off. It pays off for the individual worker, for the company, and for the industry as a whole. The other side of the training coin is downtime on the job, defective products and services, wasted materials, late deliveries, and dissatisfied customers.

Workplace know-how—the competencies and the foundation skills—offer employers a better way out. In fact, some industry organizations, such as the National Association of Manufacturers (NAM), are already beginning to focus on the SCANS message as a foundation for rethinking training needs (see Sidebar D). The competencies SCANS has defined can be taught around specific workplace tasks of interest to the sponsoring employer. Employees will

SIDEBAR D

NAM AND THE SCANS SKILLS

The National Association of Manufacturers (NAM) believes that remaining competitive in global markets will depend increasingly on the skills of the nation's workforce and the way in which human resources are used. As a result, NAM, in partnership with the Department of Labor, has created a project in workforce readiness to design innovative training models for small, medium-size, and large companies. In Phase I, focus-group research will be conducted, and in Phase II, a series of workshops will be sponsored. The purpose of the focus groups is to explore attitudes and concerns about worker readiness and current worker education and training programs among employers and employees across the country. The themes identified in the focus groups will be used in developing the workshops, which will offer hands-on examples of work-based learning as an effective method of skill acquisition. The goal is to provide a forum where local businesses can share strategies and create a network for continuing consultations.

SCANS know-how will more likely be taught in local schools if manufacturers understand the importance of these skills and competencies and then communicate that understanding to a wide range of educational institutions. Through its Association Council, which includes over 180 vertical trade associations, NAM will be a powerful vehicle for disseminating the findings about the SCANS know-how.

possess a broader set of workplace competencies and will be able to perform, in their current jobs in a superior manner.

Association-wide activities can be found in other economic sectors. The American Institute of Banking, for example, offers "Strategic Skill Builders for Banking," a package of flexible modules easily adaptable to any bank's training program. It tests participants' language and mathematics skills and offers instruction in subjects from reading to balancing cash drawers and building communications skills. The National Association of Printers and Lithographers, representing 400,000 employees, also offers extensive training. Its workplace program offers a skills inventory, manager's sourcebook, and courses in on-the-job math, communications, critical thinking, and graphic arts. The "Cafeteria Workers Skill Enhancement Training Program" is a joint labor-management program developed by the Food and Beverage

Workers with ARA Services, Inc; Canteen Corporation; Guest Services, Inc.; Marriott Corporation; Service America, Inc.; and about a dozen other food-service firms.

The ability to develop the SCANS know-how in their employees may be a matter of survival for most of the nation's small businesses (defined as those having $5 million and under in annual revenues, or 100 or fewer employees). Strategies for requiring this ability must include the development of coalitions made up of the businesses themselves, trade and professional associations, state and local government employers, and labor organizations whose members need the SCANS know-how to remain competitive (see Sidebar E for a description of a hospitality-industry coalition). The basic operational principle, of course, is synergy: What helps one helps all, and the whole becomes more than the sum of its parts.[40]

---

[40]The definition of industry extends to governance at all levels. The SCANS Government-as -Employer Task Force has prepared a report, *Government as High Performance Employer*, noted in Appendix C.

SIDEBAR E

HOSPITALITY INDUSTRY

In January 1992, 17 organizations representing the hospitality industry (including the restaurant, hotel, and tourism industries and their suppliers) met and agreed to create a Convocation of National Hospitality Industry Associations. The convocation will develop industry standards around the workplace know-how identified by SCANS.

The hospitality industry employs approximately 10 million workers. Most of the employers are members of one or more of the associations represented in the convocation. Many of the organizations have state and local chapters; combined, they make up a huge network.

The convocation's aim is to attract competent employees into the industry and to enhance education and training curriculum. The convocation adopted the following strategy:

Step 1. Define a universe of positions that are representative of the industry, including industry-specific positions (e.g., chef or restaurant manager) and support positions (e.g., executive secretary or accountant).

Step 2. Develop model descriptions for the positions identified. Each description will include a position summary; task descriptions designed around the SCANS competencies; and general qualifications including educational background, experience, and special qualifications required to perform in the position.

Step 3. Establish the required level of performance for each job task. Members of the Council on Hotel, Restaurant, and Institutional Education (CHRIE)—the leading organization involved in teaching, training and learning, research, and practice in the field of hospitality and tourism—will be asked to develop specific curriculum exercises to assess the competencies and teach them in the context of the industry.

Convocation members expect to use the standards to qualify workers seeking entry into career ladders in the hospitality industry, and to communicate these standards to all educators and schools. The convocation expects that schools teaching the SCANS know-how in the five core academic disciplines will use the curriculum exercises and assessments to teach the competencies identified by SCANS. The con-

Chapter 6
STANDARDS, ASSESSMENTS, AND CERTIFICATION

The Commission believes that achievement throughout American schools must be raised and that all students should attain the skills and knowledge needed for productive participation in the workplace of tomorrow. This task will require transforming the practices of schooling and having educators and the public at large agree on new objectives for learning and new ways of teaching and studying. It will also require developing widely understood standards of performance as well as new assessments to measure their attainment.

STANDARDS AND ASSESSMENT

Educational standards, arrived at through a public process of discussion and debate, can play a central role in reaching the needed agreement. Clearly articulated standards can communicate to everyone—teachers, students, parents—what they ought to be aiming for during the school years. The conversation can stimulate the development of high-performance schools and workplaces, and can link schools more effectively to the world of work. Above all, the standards can serve to increase the likelihood that all American young people—including the poor, minorities, and the children of immigrants—will have the opportunity to learn what they will need to know and be able to do in order to participate effectively in the nation's economy. As one SCANS

Commissioner, a critic of current standards and assessment practices, recently testified:

> American children today do not have an equal chance to learn in school. Expectations are not the same for all, the opportunities for learning are not equivalent. Almost everywhere, we expect less of children from poor and minority families; we therefore ask less of them, and, above all, we offer them less. Schools with unequal resources, formal tracking systems, and informal grouping inside classrooms create *de facto* different curricula for different groups of students. These differences are often masked by the absence of clear standards. A and B grades don't mean the same thing in different schools. Parents of poor and minority children are told that their children are doing fine, "working to their ability." How can they know that "working to ability" means working to a much lower expectation than others?
>
> Clear and public standards—the same ones for all groups of students—are the only way this situation is likely to end. With clear targets for learning for everyone, parents and advocates of poor and minority children will know exactly what should be expected of their children. And they will be able to insist that the instruction offered will allow the children to meet those expectations. Only with public, clearly understandable standards for all students can we end the double standard that is now depriving so many children of the chance to study a challenging curricu-

lum and to have access to good jobs or further education when they finish school.[41]

Many groups in the United States are participating in a continuing national conversation on standards, testing, and assessment, and there is much new activity in this area (see Sidebar F). The National Education Goals Panel endorsed the idea of a new national assessment system in 1991. The National Council on Education Standards and Testing concluded in 1992 that national standards and a "system of assessments, measuring progress toward the standards" should be put in place[42]. A foundation-funded effort with nationwide reach, the New Standards Project, is exploring how to create a "national examination system" based not on tests but on what it calls "the Three P's": student projects, portfolios of student work, and performance evaluation.

Tests Versus Assessment

Much of this new activity is a reaction to what many people term an excess of testing in our nation's schools—an activity that involves, by one estimate, at least 20 million student days, and direct expenses of 100 million tax dollars annually. Critics of our current propensity to test students repeatedly argue that today's tests (1) are designed to label, sort, and select individuals without regard to whether these tests promote learning; (2) damage test-takers by pitting students against one another in ways that result in long-lasting labels like "smart" and "dumb"; and (3) distort the educational process, because instruction often models "multiple-choice thinking" rather than critical analysis.

Experts agree that assessment is profoundly different from testing. The United States has already tried to test its way to excellence in education, and the effort has failed. By the end of the 1980s, 47 states required statewide testing, at least for minimum competence. Students, particularly low-income minority youngsters, showed modest gains in basic skills achievement, but performance in the higher-order skills required for high performance continued to be disappointing. Test results describe the problem at the end of the educational process and for that purpose they may be useful. Assessment promises to build excellence into the educational process on a day-by-day basis, rather than trying to test it in at the end.

Criteria for an Effective Assessment System

What does an assessment system need to be effective? Any system that meets the following six criteria is well on its way:[43]

1. It defines and communicates what is to be learned—that is, the outcomes that

---

[41]Summary of testimony by SCANS Commissioner Lauren Resnick before the House of Representatives' Education Subcommittee, January 1992.

[42]NCEST, *Raising Standards for American Education.*

[43]For a discussion of assessment, see Gregory R. Anrig, "National Tests: Nay. Nationwide Assessment: Yea," Testimony before House Committee on Education and Labor (March 14, 1991.) See also *Teaching the SCANS Competencies* (forthcoming) for examples of assessment items prepared by a number of the organizations listed in Sidebar F.

SIDEBAR F

PIECES OF THE STANDARDS AND ASSESSMENT PUZZLE

Several groups, organizations, and states are already at work on major elements of a new assessment system. Among the projects in progress are the following:

New Standards Project. This effort, based at the University of Pittsburgh and the National Center on Education and the Economy in Rochester, New York, is funded by the John D. and Catherine T. MacArthur Foundation and the Pew Charitable Trust. It serves as a model for much of the national standard-setting and assessment activity. The project has begun work with 17 states and local school districts around the country to show how students can be helped to achieve high standards by setting clear targets for instruction and by providing the extra help and resources to those who need them to achieve the standards.

College Entrance Examination Board. The College Board is developing Pacesetter, an array of secondary-school syllabi, related assessments, and professional development activities for teachers. The syllabi spell out for all students standards to raise student expectations and improve performance. The program is being developed in cooperation with leading disciplinary associations and educational practitioners at all levels. The initial offering in mathematics is projected for 1993, to be followed by English, world history, science, and foreign languages.

Educational Testing Service. ETS is developing WORKLINK, an electronic information system linking local schools and employers. WORKLINK is an "employer friendly" record to make school performance count in the workplace. It provides to employers (1) a reformatted high school transcript that is easy to interpret; (2) work-skills assessment covering such aptitudes as reading and using manuals, everyday math, and writing skills; (3) information on job-related behavior, including punctuality, timely work completion, and willingness to follow directions; and (4) information on work experience and out-of-school training. Students will be able to use their records as a résumé, and employers will be able to locate potential employees from a computerized WORKLINK data base managed locally. (The résumé shown in Exhibit K is based, in part, on WORKLINK.)

American College Testing Service. ACT is developing Work Keys, a system for profiling, assessing, and teaching employability skills. The system includes a series of work-related assessments covering reading, writing, computation, problem solving, and reasoning; and SCANS-like interpersonal skills (e.g., negotiation, motivation, and oral communication). Employers will profile their jobs, individuals will be profiled on skills, and instruction will be provided, all based on a Work Keys skills matrix. Work Keys is being developed in cooperation with the American Association of Community and Junior Colleges, the National Association of Community and Junior Colleges, the National Association of State Directors of Vocational/Technical Education Consortium, the National Association of Secondary School Principals, and advisory panels from five participating states.

American Council on Education. ACE, which sponsors the GED tests that permit more than 400,000 adults each year to earn a high school diploma, is developing a new, competency-based, performance-driven, assessment effort to award diplomas, the national external diploma program (EDP). Expected to be available in 1992, EDP will permit adults to demonstrate skills acquired in work and life, including many of the SCANS foundation skills and competencies: communication; problem solving; teamwork; entry-level job skills; awareness of social, public, and scientific issues; technological competence; and the ability to manipulate, synthesize, and use data in context.

State and Local Initiatives. Along with these national efforts, many states and localities are developing their own standards and replacing statewide programs of testing with assessment systems. California is one of the leading states in these efforts, along with Connecticut, Kentucky, Maryland, New York, and others. The Council of Chief State School Officers has made the "School-to-Work Transition" a top priority for the next three years and established a national consortium of states to develop new assessment systems. One group is working on work readiness. Efforts are also proceeding in local districts. The Pittsburgh Public Schools, for example, have adopted a framework of Career/Life Skill Competencies similar to SCANS, and Los Angeles will warranty that all of its graduates are proficient in the SCANS know-how.

are expected to show up in the knowledge and skills of the students. These outcomes become, in effect, standards for all. A useful assessment not merely indicates success or failure in meeting the standards but identifies the degree of progress made in meeting them.

2. It assures that students are being taught what the system calls for, and that teachers are significantly involved in determining educational standards, outcomes, and goals.

3. It permits comparison of local performance to national benchmarks.

4. It protects students against sorting and labeling by moving away from distinguishing between "good" and "bad" to measuring performance against standards of what students should know and be able to do.

5. It is dynamic, meaning it can be improved on the basis of experience and of advances in knowledge.

6. It motivates students who believe that the assessment will count in the world beyond high school because they see that employers make decisions based upon the assessment.

The Commission supports these criteria and believes it is possible to move beyond the puzzle that frustrates most assessments: how to design an assessment system that has the credibility of absolute standards built into it without penalizing students who fail to reach the standards.

DESIGNING A SYSTEM

Moving from the six criteria just listed to a fair and equitable system of standard setting and assessment requires going beyond simply creating new forms of tests. It also involves developing varied instructional opportunities and providing appropriate resources for students with special needs. (See Sidebar G for one special case, persons with limited English proficiency.) The problem is to design a system that establishes students' rights to an education up to a recognized, absolute standard of performance without putting the burden of failure on the backs of students. Here is the Commission's solution:

*   Establish for all students, beginning in middle school, a cumulative résumé. The résumé will contain information about courses taken, projects completed, and proficiency level attained in each competency. When a student reaches the performance standard for certification in a SCANS competency, that certification will be noted on the résumé. When the student has accomplished enough to meet an overall standard, the résumé will show that he or she has been awarded a certificate of initial mastery (CIM). The CIM establishes the level of achievement to which the student is entitled. It is society's obligation to provide each student with multiple opportunities to achieve the CIM in school or other settings such as youth centers or on the job. Society and student are responsible, together, for reaching the standard.

*   Students will be free to use their résumé in seeking employment or further education at any time. Employers can be expected to demand from students the highest level of certification that the job demands (e.g., high-performance workplaces can demand high skills, including—but not limited to—those required for the CIM).

*   In the near future, while only a minority of jobs are in high-performance work-

SIDEBAR G

TEACHING AND ASSESSING PERSONS WITH LIMITED ENGLISH PROFICIENCY

The United States is a nation of immigrants and is likely to remain so. The 1990 Census reports a dramatic increase in immigration from countries where Spanish or Asian and Pacific Island languages are spoken. California reports that in the future, minorities, most of whom come from immigrant families, will make up 50 to 70 percent of its population. For the 1989-90 school year, some 3 million of the children and adults in the nation's schools were classified as "limited English proficient" (LEP). At a time when the United States plays an increasing role in the global economy, the language capabilities of immigrant students and their familiarity with two cultures should be used for the benefit of all.

Whether they are enrolled in developmental or bilingual education classes, all LEP students need ongoing opportunities to combine second-language learning and literacy development with problem-solving activities. These activities should let students use the diverse knowledge they already possess. Cross-cultural comparisons should give students a chance to link their home experience with the skills needed to succeed at school and in the workplace.

LEP students can benefit from program designs and educational strategies such as the following:

- Needs assessments and diagnostics that (1) are culturally and linguistically appropriate for a given language group; (2) help evaluate the areas in which LEP students are well versed; and (3) indicate those areas where additional development is needed. These assessments must be able to distinguish problem-solving (cognitive) skills from language skills—in other words, a student may be able to perform a task but may have trouble with the English vocabulary or structures used in the directions.

- Progress assessments and performance evaluations that rely on multiple ways to measure success. Students must be provided with opportunities to demonstrate what they know and what they can do without being constantly held back by their lack of experience with the English language. For language-minority students especially, assessment must occur in many contexts.

Issues of linguistic and cultural pluralism will increase in prominence and urgency as demographic forces dramatically change the workforce. Integrating SCANS know-how with language and literacy development can provide schools and workplaces with a way to address these forces positively.

---

places, students with the CIM will naturally be more attractive to high-performance employers. (The data presented earlier in Exhibit C show that higher SCANS know-how is associated with higher-paying jobs.) As more high-performance jobs are created, the payoff for having the CIM will increase. Meanwhile, as more CIM holders become available, employers will be encouraged to create high-performance workplaces.

The proposed résumé would be a universally recognized statement of experience and accomplishment. The information would mean the same thing to everybody: this student has the SCANS know-how noted here.

The information would have this meaning because the résumé will contain more than a mere record of courses taken and grades attained—the information on a current high school transcript. Beginning in middle school, each student would accumulate a record of port-folios, projects completed, teacher evaluations, project samples, assessment results, and the like. As students reach higher and higher levels of performance for any particular subject matter or SCANS competency, the fact will be noted in the résumé. (See Exhibit K for a hypothetical résumé.)

The benefits of such a résumé for student and employee are considerable: For the student, the résumé becomes a permanent record of genuine attainment. As more and more high-performance jobs require higher and higher competence, the résumé will have a more obvious payoff for the student. Employers will benefit from the realistic expectation that their businesses can demand higher levels of competency, and become high-performance workplaces.

In the Commission's view, it is essential that the certification system incorporate the other part of the equation—avoiding penalties for students who fail to reach the standards. The Commission advocates world-class standards. Initially, many students can be expected to fall short, and, as we have said, the burden of that failure should not be placed solely on the backs of students.

If the new assessment system is to work equitably, students and workers should be *entitled* to multiple opportunities to acquire the competence needed to earn a decent living. The Commission believes that society has an obligation to balance the demand for high standards with a commitment to help all young peo-

ple attain them. That is, schools and the workplace should offer multiple chances to work toward the standard—in school, in skills centers, in youth programs, and on the job.

The Commission believes that most students will earn their certificate of initial mastery by age 16, but no age limit should be imposed. Students may take as long as they need, and the schools will be obliged to provide education that enables students to acquire the certificate, and to provide the services necessary for students of any age, both in-school and out-of-school, to meet this goal. Thus the system is not "pass/fail" but "ready/try again."

The levels of performance required for a CIM should be benchmarked to the highest standard in the world for 16-year-olds. They should be chosen on the basis of estimates of the skills needed to succeed in further education and to participate productively in the workplace of tomorrow. Under today's civil rights law, many employers will be barred from using the CIM as a ticket for job selection because their jobs do not need all the skills that the CIM will certify. But some advanced workplaces do need workers with all these skills, and these are the jobs with the best pay and the best chances for career advancement. All employers could, however, review all of the other information on the résumé. Consistent with civil rights law, they could match the qualifications evident on the résumé with the level and mix of skills needed for the jobs they have available.

The knowledge that the chances of securing a good job are significantly increased

EXHIBIT K

HYPOTHETICAL RÉSUMÉ

Jane Smith
19 Main Street
Anytown
Home Phone: (817) 777-3333

Date of Report: 5/1/92
Soc. Sec.: 599-46-1234
Date of Birth: 3/7/73
Age: 19

SCANS Workplace Competency	Date	Proficiency Level
Resources	10/91	1
Interpersonal Skills	12/91	2
Information	11/92	3
Technology	1/92	2
Systems	4/92	3

Core Academic and Elective Courses	Date	Proficiency Level
English	11/91	3
Mathematics	12/91	3
Science	2/91	3
History	4/91	2
Geography	8/91	1
Fine Arts	11/91	4
Vocational/Industrial Education	4/92	2

SCANS Personal Qualities	Average Rating	No. of Ratings
Responsibility	Excellent	10
Self-Esteem	Excellent	10
Sociability	Excellent	8
Self-Management	Excellent	7
Integrity/Honesty	Good	6

Portfolios and Other Materials Available		Reference
1.	Report on Grounds Keeping (Chemistry)	Mr. Kent
2.	Video on Architectural Styles (Social Studies)	Ms. Jones
3.	Newspaper Article Written	Ms. French

Extracurricular Activities	Role	Date	Reference
Newspaper	Reporter	9/89–1/90	Frank Jones (Adviser)
Basketball Varsity	Center	9/90–6/91	Dean Smith (Coach)

Awards and Honors	Date	Source	Reference
Teen Volunteer of the Year	6/91	Rotary Club	John Grove
Class Secretary	9/91–1/92	Lincoln High School	Emma Rice

(continued)

Points Toward Certificate of Initial Mastery		Earned 300	Required 500
(Supplied by Student)			
Work Experience	**Date**	**Place**	**Reference**
Volunteer Work	6/88–6/89	St. Joseph Homeless Shelter	Father John O'Connell (508) 296-3304
Summer Camp Counselor	6/91–8/87	Camp Kiowa	Susan Miller (508) 628-5128
Office (Word Processor)	1/90–5/92	PDQ Secretarial Help	Myrna Copper (508) 389-0202

by certification will motivate students to work toward acquiring the necessary skills (and to prod their parents to put pressure on the schools to improve students' ability to do so). Because this information would be extremely useful to employers in making hiring decisions and to colleges in evaluating applications, students would have a strong motivation to learn the SCANS foundation skills and workplace competencies, and employers and colleges would have a strong incentive to require them. It would be up to the consumers of this information, whether employers, colleges, the military, or others, to decide on what weight to give each element in the résumé, using their own needs as guides.

DEVELOPING STANDARDS FOR SCANS COMPETENCIES

Neither the résumé nor the obligation of society to educate students will mean much unless clear standards of student performance come to be widely accepted by teachers, parents, school leaders, businesses, and communities. These standards cannot be imposed from above or afar, but must come to pervade education because they are the internalized goals of everyone working in it. They must be high standards that prepare students well for good jobs in the economy of the future.

The process of developing standards must be public and involve a wide set of parties. Educators, employers, parents, workers, and students must come to common understandings of how competent school performance can be related to performance on the job. Standards should be developed by states and localities, but benchmarked to national and international standards. A system to certify that these standards (and the assessments that go with them) meet these benchmarks is needed to ensure the "portability" of credentials.

The National Council on Education Standards and Testing recommended in January 1992 that the SCANS competencies be integrated into standards developed for academic subjects. We hope that the curriculum-development work of several groups—the National Council of Teachers of Mathematics, the National Council of Teachers of English, the National Science Teachers Association, and others—will follow the council's advice. Otherwise, SCANS competencies will be taught in separate tracks, and the opportunity for an integrated education of equal quality for all children will have been missed.

Clear and high standards of performance should meet several criteria: (1) They must be publicly and widely discussed and locally set; educators, trainers, employers, labor organizations, and the public at large should fully understand the standards. (2) Teachers and trainers must know what they are expected to accomplish. (3) Students, workers, and parents must understand what is expected of them. And (4) school systems and government should know what is required of them.

This Commission has begun the process of developing standards for the SCANS know-how by specifying the content of the knowledge and skills that schools should teach. We have expressed this content at two levels.[44] Our first, overarching statement for each competency area was contained in *What Work Requires of Schools* and is repeated in Appendix B of this document. A more detailed description of the required content will be available in a companion volume to this report, *Teaching the SCANS Competencies*.[45] Further work will be required to develop content standards appropriate to all levels of schooling.

The next step in standard setting is to establish expected levels of student performance in the subject matter. For example, as we stated in our initial report, this Commission believes that every student leaving school should be able to demonstrate certain foundation skills at the following level:

- **Read and write** well enough to handle records, memoranda, and correspondence without difficulty; locate, understand, and interpret written information; and communicate ideas clearly and concisely in writing, using prose, graphs, and charts as required.

- **Understand mathematics** well enough to make simple computations, estimate results, interpret and develop diagrams and charts, work with computer programs, and apply mathematics in real-world situations (such as estimating unit costs or volume discounts).

- **Speak clearly and persuasively** as the job requires—responding to complaints, making group presentations, and asking questions when instructions are unclear or competing job requirements are ambiguous.

- **Listen** carefully to understand messages, to benefit from time in training spent, and to pick up the motivations and hidden messages of customers, clients, co-workers, or supervisors .

---

[44]See NCEST, *Raising Standards for American Education.*

[45]See Appendix C for more information about this publication and about its companion volume, *Skills and Tasks for Jobs.*

Defining complete performance standards for the foundation skills requires agreement on the types of records, memoranda, correspondence, graphs, charts, and so on that are meant in these statements.

It is the judgment of the Commission that student performance standards should be set at a level sufficient to enable all students to earn a decent living. Our data (see Exhibit C in Chapter 2) suggest that this means reaching at least the midpoint of the five levels of difficulty shown in the scales contained in *Skills and Tasks for Jobs*. Examples of tasks at this level are shown in Exhibit L. These represent the standards required for successful entry into positions that have a career ladder or other opportunity for advancement associated with them.

It is important, however, to recognize that different jobs require different skills. Therefore it is not necessary—and indeed would violate recent civil rights legislation—to require every applicant for every role to achieve at the third level in every skill. As one Commissioner stated, "The analogy is to the decathlon. I made up in running the hurdles what I lost in the shot-put." The principle stated in Chapter 3 holds— all Americans should have multiple opportunities to attain proficiency in the SCANS know-how at a level sufficient to earn a decent living. The mix of skills required will vary according to the career aspirations of individual students. What is important is that each person must have the opportunity to attain some set of skills at a sufficiently high level of performance to obtain a good job and earn a decent living.

EXHIBIT L

TASKS FROM DIVERSE OCCUPATIONS REPRESENTATIVE OF LEVEL OF PERFORMANCE IN SCANS KNOW-HOW REQUIRED FOR ENTRY INTO JOBS WITH CAREER LADDER

	TASK				
Resources	**Travel Agent:** Sets priorities for work tasks on a daily basis so that travel arrangements are completed in a timely manner.	**Chef:** Prepares weekly sales projections—conducts inventory of food supplies; calculates the costs of purchased and on-hand food; determines sales.	**Medical Assistant:** Acquires, maintains, and tracks supplies on hand—inventories supplies and equipment, fills out reorder forms, and obtains extra supplies when merchandise is on sale.	**Quality Control Inspector:** Establishes a system for inspecting elevators within a given area and time frame while allowing for other contingencies.	**Chef:** Performs a cost analysis on menu items in order to turn a profit.
Interpersonal Skills	**Child-Care Aide:** Works as a member of a team in the classroom.	**Outside Equipment Technician:** Coordinates with a peer technician to install a point-to-point data circuit in two different cities.	**Carpenter:** Shares experiences and knowledge with other workers, and cooperates with others on a variety of tasks to accomplish project goals.	**Accounting/Financial Analyst:** Teaches a co-worker the procedure for sending bimonthly memos.	**Customer Service Representative:** Assists customers in selecting merchandise or resolving complaints.
Information	**Travel Agent:** Uses on-line computer terminal to retrieve information relating to customer requests, plans itinerary, and books airline tickets.	**Blue-Collar Worker Supervisor:** Records and maintains purchase requests, purchase invoices, and cost information on raw materials.	**Child-care Aide:** Compiles accurate written records including all facets of the child's play for the office and the parents.	**Order-Filler:** Communicates a down-time situation to co-workers, and explains the situation so that everyone can visualize and understand it.	**Cosmetologist:** Keeps abreast of new and emerging styles and techniques through magazines and attendance at fashion shows.
Systems	**Medical Assistant:** Understands the systems of the organization and the organization's ultimate goal (i.e., excellent patient care).	**Accounting/Financial Analyst:** Performs analyses comparing current expenditures with projected needs and revenues.	**Shipping and Receiving Clerk:** Unloads and directs material throughout the plant to storage and the assembly line in accordance with company policy.	**Food Service Worker:** Evaluates the performance of workers and adjusts work assignments to increase staff efficiency.	**Plastic Molding Machine Operator:** Monitors gauges and dials to ensure that the machine operates at the proper rate of speed.

(continued)

EXHIBIT L
(Continued)

TASKS FROM DIVERSE OCCUPATIONS REPRESENTATIVE OF LEVEL OF PERFORMANCE IN SCANS KNOW-HOW REQUIRED FOR ENTRY INTO JOBS WITH CAREER LADDER

	TASK				
Technology	**Travel Agent:** Uses the on-line computer terminal to retrieve information relating to the customer's request, plan the itinerary, and book the airline ticket.	**Accounting/Financial Analyst:** Prepares the monthly debt schedule, including reviews of financial statements.	**Expeditor/Purchasing Agent:** Accesses the computer to retrieve required forms used to request bids and to place purchase orders.	**Industry Training Specialist:** Uses available computer and video technology to enhance the realism of training and to conserve time.	**Order Filler:** Operates a forklift and ensures that it is in proper operating condition.
Basic Skills	**Dental Hygienist:** Reads professional manuals to understand issues related to new techniques and equipment.	**Sales Representative, Hotel Services:** Assesses client accounts to determine adherence to company standards.	**Optician:** Measures a customer's facial features to calculate bifocal segment heights.	**Law Enforcement Officer:** Prepares written reports of incidents and crimes.	**Contractor:** Prepares a letter to a subcontractor delineating responsibilities for completion of an earth-grading contract.
Thinking Skills	**Expeditor/Purchasing Agent:** Decides what supplier to use during a bid evaluation based on supplier information stored in the computer.	**Blue-Collar Worker Supervisor:** Sets priorities for processing orders to resolve a conflict in scheduling.	**Truck Delivery Salesperson/Outside Sales:** Collects money from delinquent customers and uses judgment on extending credit.	**Contractor:** Analyzes and corrects the problem when timber piles break before reaching specified bearing loads.	**Travel Agent:** Compensates a customer who is dissatisfied with his or her travel experience.
Personal Qualities	**Optician:** Responds appropriately to customer requests, demonstrates understanding of customer needs, and exhibits friendliness and politeness to customers.	**Quality Control Inspector:** Performs independent research to assess compliance.	**Computer Operator:** Assumes responsibility for the arrangement and completion of jobs run on the mainframe.	**Telemarketing Representative:** Displays a sense of concern and interest in customers' business and company.	**Sales Representative, Hotel Services:** Asserts self and networks with people at conventions in order to obtain hotel business.

Source: *Skills and Tasks for Jobs.*

CONCLUSION
A LEARNING-A-LIVING SYSTEM

As we said in our first report and again in this one, the Commission understands that preparation for work is only part of the mission of schools. We also recognize that school is only part of the learning process. President Bush has spoken of the need for America to be a nation of learners and for the "education revolution" to extend beyond the schools into the community. Achieving this goal requires that every community build a system that clearly connects learning with earning a living.

COMMUNITY PARTICIPANTS

The National Urban League, which has for years served as an education resource to the minority community, prepared Exhibit M for the Commission. It illustrates that the community—parents, teachers, employers and community-based organizations, such as the Urban League—all play a role in developing high-performance learners and workers. These community members must work together if the SCANS goals are to be achieved.

Schools will have to reinvent themselves to teach the SCANS competencies. Employers, public and private, will have to assess the SCANS know-how of their work force and develop training strategies to improve their employees' competency.

The Federal Government will have to finance research and development and mea-

sure the nation's progress toward high performance. In this regard, SCANS is pleased to note that the Departments of Labor and Education and the Office of Personnel Management have joined in a multiyear project to develop SCANS assessment measures, making it possible to include the SCANS competencies in the National Assessment of Educational Progress (NAEP).

CONNECTING LEARNING AND EARNING

Every community must have a coherent system to ease the transition between school and work for youngsters and to foster lifelong learning for adults. The SCANS efforts have been directed to providing our communities with a tool for building such systems: a language to connect education and work. Such a common language is needed if all participants are to have the information they need. Agreement on the SCANS language will facilitate the flow of information in the "learning a living" system as shown in Exhibit N.

The box on the left side of Exhibit N represents formal education. Within it, instruction in the SCANS workplace competencies and foundation skills is integrated with the academic curriculum until at least the junior year of high school. Students learn the SCANS know-how in English, math, science, history, and geography, in other classes (e.g., art), and in extracurricular activities.

The basic idea is that all students follow a common academic program, a single track, until they are about 16. After age 16, some students are more likely to be learning the SCANS competencies in the more specialized contexts of work, perhaps even specializing in an industry such as manufacturing or hospitality. Some of these students will spend their last two years in high school in a "2+2 tech-prep program" that will conclude with two years in a community college and an associate degree. Other students will continue to learn SCANS competencies in academic courses as they move toward a four-year college program. Still others will go directly to work after high school graduation and participate in work-based learning, including apprenticeship.

The box on the right side of Exhibit N represents employers and work-based educa-

EXHIBIT M

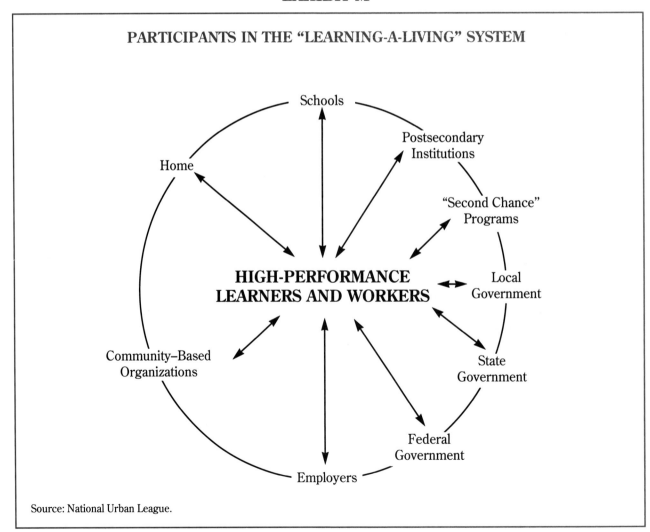

PARTICIPANTS IN THE "LEARNING-A-LIVING" SYSTEM

Schools

Postsecondary
Institutions

"Second Chance"
Programs

Home

**HIGH-PERFORMANCE
LEARNERS AND WORKERS**

Local
Government

Community–Based
Organizations

State
Government

Federal
Government

Employers

Source: National Urban League.

tion. This box includes the human resource functions of recruiting, developing, and retaining employees. It also includes learning that continues for a lifetime and is usually done while learners are employed. Workplace education produces portable certificates that are valued in many workplaces.

Information flows from employers to educators through recruiting and employee development activities, including the ways in which employees progress up career ladders.

Employers tell educators "what work requires of school." Educators, in their turn, inform employers of the competencies that students have attained. Teachers certify "what students know and can do."

Students move easily from school-based learning to work-based learning, or from high school to a variety of postsecondary certificate-granting institutions. Such institutions include four-year and community colleges, proprietary schools, and employer-union offerings of work-

EXHIBIT N

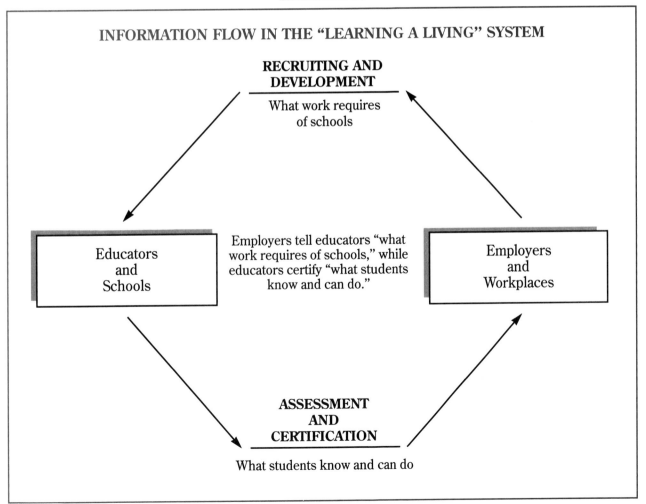

INFORMATION FLOW IN THE "LEARNING A LIVING" SYSTEM

RECRUITING AND
DEVELOPMENT

What work requires
of schools

Educators
and
Schools

Employers tell educators "what
work requires of schools," while
educators certify "what students
know and can do."

Employers
and
Workplaces

ASSESSMENT
AND
CERTIFICATION

What students know and can do

site learning. Dropouts enter the "second chance" system. Some immigrants who have come to the United States past high school age take "remedial" or "developmental" classes. Members of these groups are able to proceed to postsecondary work.

A lifelong learning system serves all adults, including those who lack basic education skills, and adults who did not complete high school. Instead of having to enroll in programs labeled "basic literacy," these adults are offered courses that teach literacy and other basic skills in the context of job requirements for the SCANS competencies.[46]

Job referral organizations connect students with jobs and with education for careers. These organizations use the SCANS language to integrate the three languages that are used today: those of the academic high school (algebra and American history), employers (résumés), and education providers involved in vocational preparation (welding and auto repair).

The referral organization assesses students' skills and knowledge, knows the skills required for jobs, understands the future prospects for jobs and firms in their labor markets, and refers clients to some combination of employment and educational program.[47] The referral organization also helps students to enter a career track and helps employers to build high-performance workplaces.

In the learning-a-living system, assessment of adults, either on the job or outside work, is not based on existing instruments such as the Test of Adult Basic Education (TABE) or grade-level reading tests. Instead, referral agencies or employers are able to assess the SCANS competencies within a relatively short time, giving adults credit for accomplishments in previous employment. High school students receive college credit for Advanced Placement courses; adults take credit for demonstrated competence in the SCANS know-how.

The foregoing paragraphs do not describe today's earning-a-living system, in which neither employers nor educators receive or deliver information effectively. The SCANS aim is to improve the information flow—and the learning and the earning—so that the economy will deliver the high rates of productivity and wage increases that characterized the United States in the years from 1937 to 1973.

BUILDING THE SYSTEM

The work of the Secretary's Commission on Achieving Necessary Skills involved two issues that are part of any serious consideration about life in the United States in the 21st century: an improved education system and a more productive national economy. Our findings and recommendations provide a blueprint for linking these two in a way that will reward our people

---

[46]Thomas Sticht, "Adult Literacy Education," *Review of Research in Education*, vol. 15 (1988/89).

[47]The skill centers proposed by the Administration in *Job Training 2000* constitute an attempt to establish such a referral system.

with an improved standard of living. The outcomes that are needed are shown in Exhibit O. Unless the nation takes forceful action on this agenda, the nation's schools, employers, students, and workers will not prosper in the next century.

We hope that this, our final report, provides a blueprint that communities at the national, state, and local levels can and will use. Each community must decide what resources will be allocated to create a system that will meet its specific goals. But first, each community must become involved in a conversation about its place in a fast-changing world as we approach the year 2000. Our nation's ability to lead in a global economy will depend on the outcome of those conversations. This Commission is confident that once communities are informed, citizens will commit themselves to maintaining the American dream for themselves and their children.

EXHIBIT O

RECOMMENDATIONS FOR THE "LEARNING A LIVING" SYSTEM

**THE COMMISSION RECOMMENDS FULL IMPLEMENTATION
OF THE FOLLOWING ACTIONS BY THE YEAR 2000:**

Reinventing Schools

- Workplace know-how (the SCANS foundation and workplace competencies) should be taught along the entire continuum of education, from kindergarten through college.

- Every student should complete middle school (about age 14) with an introduction to workplace know-how.

- Every student by about age 16 should attain initial mastery of the SCANS know-how.

- Every student should complete high school sufficiently proficient in the SCANS know-how to earn a decent living.

- All federally funded programs for youth and adults, including vocational education programs, should teach the SCANS know-how.

Fostering Work-Based Learning

- Federal agencies should incorporate SCANS workplace competencies into their own employee programs.

- Private-sector work-based training programs should incorporate training in the SCANS workplace competencies.

- Coalitions of businesses, associations, government employers, and labor organizations should teach the SCANS competencies to the current workforce, including employees of small businesses.

Reorganizing the Workplace

- The vast majority of employers should adopt the standards of quality and high performance that now characterize our most competitive companies.

- Companies should develop internal training programs to bring employees to the proficiency in the SCANS competencies needed for high-performance work organizations.

Restructuring Assessment

- A national education-based assessment system should be implemented that will permit educational institutions to certify the levels of the SCANS competencies that their students have achieved.

- Public and private employers should define requirements for higher-level competencies.

- Employment-based assessments should permit diagnoses of individual learning needs.

APPENDIX A
ACKNOWLEDGMENTS

The Secretary's Commission on Achieving Necessary Skills (SCANS) will go out of existence in April 1992, just two years since it was launched in mid-May of 1990. It has been a true working Commission. Together with an outstanding staff led by its executive director, Arnold Packer, we have labored to deal with a complex set of intellectually challenging, intertwined, and potentially emotional issues. Each Commissioner served and worked on an industry task force and on a committee related to one of the issues dealt with in this report. Although there was much heated debate, none of it was ideological; indeed, the representatives of business, labor, and education were more often challenging than defending their own communities.

SCANS was conceived by Roberts T. Jones, Assistant Secretary of the Employment and Training Administration (ETA). He and then-Secretary of Labor Elizabeth Dole created the Commission. Success would not have been possible without the continued and energetic support of Secretary Lynn Martin over more than half of the Commission's existence. In addition, Raymond J. Uhalde and Sally Jo Vasicko of ETA have been most supportive of the Commission's efforts.

Arnold Packer has been more than executive director, for his parentage of the seminal study *Workforce 2000* laid the cornerstone of the reform structure we continue to assemble. His intellect, commitment, dedication, and leadership underlie all that we present in this effort.

The Commission's work could not have been accomplished without the exceptional effort of the research contractors. Michael Kane, project director for Pelavin Associates, the prime contractor for this effort, coordinated the work of the several organizations involved, helped the Commission shape its ideas, and worked long into the night to put them into words. Norman Peterson of the American Institutes for Research designed and led the field research. Sol Pelavin and David Goslin, presidents of these two research organizations, were personally and productively involved, as was Sue Berryman at the Institute for Education and the Economy. James Harvey, of James Harvey Associates, wrote the drafts that gave this document its structure. Finally, Scott Widmeyer and Kevin Bonderud of The Widmeyer Group helped the Commission disseminate its results to the public at large and especially to the education community. Others who have assisted are listed on the following page.

A great debt of gratitude is owed to the SCANS staff, especially John Wirt, deputy director, who brought his knowledge of education to the Commission and to the topic of assessment, one of the most intellectually challenging issues that SCANS addressed. Ambrose Bittner worked closely with the labor and government-as-employer task forces and Roland Brack with the education task force and community organizations. Consuelo Ricart is the reason why there is a Spanish-language version of *What Work Requires of Schools* and why such notable progress has been made by the associations from the hospitality industry. Michael Schmidt, on loan from OPM, was extremely helpful. Patsy Terhune kept the entire effort on task.

Finally, I have truly relished my association with all those who have been involved in the process, those who are mentioned, and all who have called and written to encourage, guide, or correct our efforts.

William E. Brock

William E. Brock
Chairman

ADDITIONAL KEY STAFF

- **Department of Labor:** Kimball Baker, Diane P. Davis, Gerri Fiala, Bonnie Friedman, Allison Goddard, Elaine Golla, John Hawk, Bryan Keilty, Ronald Rubbin, Shirley M. Smith, and David O. Williams

- **Occupational Analysis Field Centers:** Paul Cleary, Boston, Massachusetts; Tom Kearney, Detroit; Stanley M. Rose, Raleigh, North Carolina; Barbara Smith, Salt Lake City; and Gerome Stevens, St. Louis, Missouri

- **Pelavin Associates, Inc.:** Ann Meltzer, deputy project director; Nancy Matheson; Tom White; Carol Copple; Gwen Pegram; and Jo Ann Blue

- **American Institutes for Research:** Deborah Whetzel, Scott Oppler, and Roselda Henry

- **National Alliance of Business:** Louise Bertsche

- **The Widmeyer Group:** Phyllis Blaunstein, Edward Fiske, and Doug Smith

- **James Harvey and Associates:** Bruce Boston and Frank Harvey

- **Frost Associates:** Hugh Frost

- **Research and Evaluation Associates:** Sherrita Porter

EMPLOYERS

Many companies and employees generously contributed their time to the job analysis research conducted by the Commission;

AAA Auto Club, World Wide Travel; Alan K. Jorgenson Construction; Alexandria Police Department; Aetna; American Empress; American Institutes for Research; ARA Food Service; Arlington County Police Department; Arthur Andersen & Company; AVX Corporation; Bally's Casino Resorts Reno; Beauty Boutique; Bell Atlantic Network; Bogart; Bowen Engineering Corporation; C&P Telephone Company; Cactus Cantina; Cafe Atlantico; Carolina Power & Light; Carousel Square Food Service; Carpenter's District Council; Carr Printing Company; Chrysler Motors; Cigna; Clarion Hotel; Confidential; Farmers National Bank; Co-operative Optical Services; Cooper Tools/Lufkin; D.C. General Hospital; Dayton-Hudson Corporation; Dearborn Federal Credit Union; Federal Express; Fete Accomplie; GE Aircraft Systems; Greater Southeast Community Hospital; Group Health Association; Hyatt Regency; International Brotherhood of Electrical Workers; M. Hall Stanton Elementary School; Marriott Corporation; Maryland Department of Licensing and Regulation; MB Graphics; MCI; Mildred D. Monroe Elementary School; National Security Agency; National Joint Apprenticeship and Training Committee; Nordstrom; Ross Dress for Less; Sheraton Park Avenue; Sibley Memorial Hospital; Sovran Bank; St. Joseph's Hospital; TGI Friday's; The Hartford; The News Journal; Truland; University of North Carolina at Chapel Hill Dental School; United Parcel Service; Wacovia Bank; and Westmore Elementary School.

79

EXPERTS

Curtis Banks, Howard University; Henry Braun, Educational Testing Service; Cynthia Brown, Council of Chief State School Officers; Gordon Cawelti, Association for Supervision and Curriculum Development; Marilyn Gowing, Office of Personnel Management; Robert Guion, Bowling Green University; Joseph P. Hickey, Council of State Governments; Edward Keller, National Association of Elementary School Principals; Thomas Koerner, National Association of Secondary School Principals; Martharose Laffey, National School Boards Association; Alan Lesgold, University of Pittsburgh; Richard D. Miller, American Association of School Administrators; Jane Pines, Human Resources Development Institute; Terry Rosen, American Federation of State, County and Municipal Employees; Lenore Saltman, Department of Defense; Joan Seamon, U. S. Department of Education; Kate Snider, American Association of Colleges of Teacher Education; Candace Sullivan, National Association of State Boards of Education; and Joan Wills, Institute for Educational Leadership.

APPENDIX B
DEFINITIONS OF SCANS KNOW-HOW

WORKPLACE COMPETENCIES

RESOURCES

Manages Time—Selects relevant, goal-related activities, ranks them in order of importance, allocates time to activities, and understands, prepares, and follows schedules.

Manages Money—Uses or prepares budgets, including making cost and revenue forecasts; keeps detailed records to track budget performance; and makes appropriate adjustments.

Manages Material and Facility Resources—Acquires, stores, and distributes materials, supplies, parts, equipment, space, or final products in order to make the best use of them.

Manages Human Resources—Assesses knowledge and skills, distributes work accordingly, evaluates performance, and provides feedback.

INTERPERSONAL

Participates as a Member of a Team—Works cooperatively with others and contributes to group efforts with ideas, suggestions, and effort.

Teaches Others—Helps others learn needed knowledge and skills.

Serves Clients/Customers—Works and communicates with clients and customers to satisfy their expectations.

Exercises Leadership—Communicates thoughts, feelings, and ideas to justify a position, encourage, persuade, convince, or otherwise motivate an individual or groups, including responsibly challenging existing procedures, policies, or authority.

Negotiates to Arrive at a Decision—Works towards an agreement that may involve exchanging specific resources or resolving divergent interests.

Works with Cultural Diversity—Works well with men and women and with people from a variety of ethnic, social, or educational backgrounds.

INFORMATION

Acquires and Evaluates Information—Identifies a need for data, obtains the data from existing sources or creates them, and evaluates their relevance and accuracy.

Organizes and Maintains Information—Organizes, processes, and maintains written or computerized records and other forms of information in a systematic fashion.

Interprets and Communicates Information—Selects and analyzes information and communicates the results to others using oral, written, graphic, pictorial, or multimedia methods.

Uses Computers to Process Information—Employs computers to acquire, organize, analyze, and communicate information.

SYSTEMS

Understands Systems—Knows how social, organizational, and technological systems work and operates effectively within them.

Monitors and Corrects Performance—Distinguishes trends, predicts impacts of actions on system operations, diagnoses deviations in the functioning of a system/organization, and takes necessary action to correct performance.

Improves and Designs Systems—Makes suggestions to modify existing systems in order to improve the quality of products or services and develops new or alternative systems.

TECHNOLOGY

Selects Technology—Judges which sets of procedures, tools, or machines, including computers and their programs, will produce the desired results.

Applies Technology to Task—Understands the overall intents and the proper procedures for setting up and operating machines, including computers and their programming systems.

Maintains and Troubleshoots Technology—Prevents, identifies, or solves problems in machines, computers, and other technologies.

THE FOUNDATION SKILLS

BASIC SKILLS

Reading—Locates, understands, and interprets written information in prose and documents—including manuals, graphs, and schedules—to perform tasks; learns from text by determining the main idea or essential message; identifies relevant details, facts, and specifications; infers or locates the meaning of unknown or technical vocabulary; and judges the accuracy, appropriateness, style, and plausibility of reports, proposals, or theories of other writers.

Writing—Communicates thoughts, ideas, information, and messages in writing; records information completely and accurately; composes and creates documents such as letters, directions, manuals, reports, proposals, graphs, and flow charts with the language, style, organization, and format appropriate to the subject matter, purpose, and audience; includes, where appropriate, supporting documentation, and attends to level of detail; and checks, edits, and revises for correct information, appropriate emphasis, form, grammar, spelling, and punctuation.

Arithmetic—Performs basic computations; uses basic numerical concepts such as whole numbers and percentages in practical situations; makes reasonable estimates of arithmetic results without a calculator; and uses tables, graphs, diagrams, and charts to obtain or convey quantitative information.

Mathematics—Approaches practical problems by choosing appropriately from a variety of mathematical techniques; uses quantitative data to construct logical explanations for real world situations; expresses mathematical ideas and concepts orally and in writing; and understands the role of chance in the occurrence and prediction of events.

Listening—Receives, attends to, interprets, and responds to verbal messages and other cues such as body language in ways that are appropriate to the purpose—for example, to comprehend, learn, critically evaluate, appreciate, or support the speaker.

Speaking—Organizes ideas and communicates oral messages appropriate to listeners and situations; participates in conversation, discussion, and group presentations; selects an appropriate medium for conveying a message; uses verbal language and other cues such as body language in a way appropriate in style, tone, and level of complexity to the audience and the occasion; speaks clearly and communicates a message; understands and responds to listener feedback; and asks questions when needed.

THINKING SKILLS

Creative Thinking—Generates new ideas by making nonlinear or unusual connections, changing or reshaping goals, and imagining new possibilities; and uses imagination freely, combining ideas or information in new ways, making connections between seemingly unrelated ideas, and reshaping goals in ways that reveal new possibilities.

Decision Making—Specifies goals and constraints, generates alternatives, considers risks, and evaluates and chooses best alternatives.

Problem Solving—Recognizes that a problem exists (i.e., that there is a discrepancy between what is and what should be); identifies possible reasons for the discrepancy, and devises and implements a plan of action to resolve it; and evaluates and monitors progress, revising the plan as indicated by findings.

Mental Visualization—Sees things in the mind's eye by organizing and processing symbols, pictures, graphs, objects, or other information—for example, sees a building from a blueprint, a system's operation from schematics, the flow of work activities from narrative descriptions, or the taste of food from reading a recipe.

Knowing How to Learn—Recognizes and can use learning techniques to apply and adapt existing and new knowledge and skills in both familiar and changing situations; and is aware of learning tools such as personal learning styles (visual, aural, etc.), formal learning strategies (notetaking or clustering items that share some characteristics), and informal learning strategies (awareness of unidentified false assumptions that may lead to faulty conclusions).

Reasoning—Discovers a rule or principle underlying the relationship between two or more objects and applies it in solving a problem—for example, uses logic to draw conclusions from available information, extracts rules or principles from a set of objects or a written text, or applies rules and principles to a new situation (or determines which conclusions are correct when given a set of facts and conclusions).

PERSONAL QUALITIES

Responsibility—Exerts a high level of effort and perseverance toward goal attainment; works hard to become excellent at doing tasks by setting high standards, paying attention to details, working well even when assigned an unpleasant task, and displaying a high level of concentration; and displays high standards of attendance, punctuality, enthusiasm, vitality, and optimism in approaching and completing tasks.

Self-Esteem—Believes in own self-worth and maintains a positive view of self, demonstrates knowledge of own skills and abilities, is aware of one's impression on others, and knows own emotional capacity and needs and how to address them.

Sociability—Demonstrates understanding, friendliness, adaptability, empathy, and politeness in new and ongoing group settings; asserts self in familiar and unfamiliar social situations; relates well to others; responds appropriately as the situation requires; and takes an interest in what others say and do.

Self-Management—Accurately assesses own knowledge, skills, and abilities; sets well-defined and realistic personal goals; monitors progress toward goal attainment and motivates self through goal achievement; and exhibits self-control and responds to feedback unemotionally and nondefensively.

Integrity/Honesty—Recognizes when being faced with making a decision or exhibiting behavior that may break with commonly held personal or societal values; understands the effects of violating these beliefs and codes on an organization, oneself, and others; and chooses an ethical course of action.

APPENDIX C
OTHER SCANS MATERIAL

More information about the topics covered in this report is available from the U.S. Government Printing Office (GPO). You can order what you need by using the form on page 87.

LEARNING A LIVING: A BLUEPRINT FOR HIGH PERFORMANCE—PART I

Part I of this document is available as a separate publication. Part I summarizes why change is needed in our schools and workplaces, identifies three parts of the learning system that must change, and lists the main recommendations of the report. (36 pages)

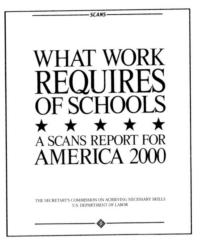

WHAT WORK REQUIRES OF SCHOOLS

The initial SCANS report is also available from GPO. The report defines the five competencies and three-part foundation that constitute the SCANS know-how. The five competencies are allocating resources, working with others, using information, understanding systems, and using technology. (61 pages)

LO QUE TRABAJO NECESITA DE LAS ESCUELAS

This is the Spanish version of *What Work Requires of Schools.*

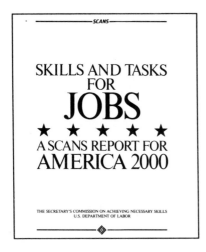

SKILLS AND TASKS FOR JOBS

This SCANS report is designed as a resource for educators or employers to use in developing curriculum for teaching the SCANS competencies and foundation skills, or for persons who counsel "students" in schools and workplaces. It consists of all the descriptive information obtained by SCANS in its job analysis. (535 pages)

The job task information is presented in two ways: First, the tasks for each SCANS competency and foundation skill are listed, and scaled by level of difficulty. Then, the tasks are listed by job for each of the 50 jobs for which data were collected. There are over 900 tasks in the volume.

TEACHING THE SCANS COMPETENCIES

This report provides expanded definitions of the five SCANS competencies as well as key concepts involved in incorporating them into the school curriculum. A section of approximately 10 pages is devoted to each competency. Other resources for integrating the competencies in the teaching of core subjects are identified. In addition examples of teaching the SCANS competencies or engaging in skill identification efforts are drawn from 27 different schools, apprenticeship, and business-education par ship programs. Another chapter describes t IndianaPLUS Program. There is also a chapter devoted to teaching SCANS to students with limited English proficiency. Finally, some sample assessment items are included. (180 pages)

SECOND TO NONE

A videotape on SCANS, *Second to None*, is available for sale from the National Audiovisual Center, 8700 Edgeworth Drive, Capitol Heights, MD, 20743-3701. Tel. (301) 763-1850. The tape is one-half hour long and costs $45.00 per copy.

To order these reports, complete the order form on the following page (You may send a photocopy instead.)

To order additional copies please use the order form below.

- -

Superintendent of Documents Order Form

Order Processing Code: *** 3102**

Charge your order.
It's Easy!
MasterCard   VISA

☐ **YES**, please send me the following publications:

To fax your orders (202) 512–2250

Qty.	Stock Number	Title	Price Each
	029-000-00439-1	Learning A Living, Part I	$2.50
	029-000-00440-4	Learning A Living, Full Report	$6.50
	029-000-00433-1	What Work Requires of Schools	$3.25
	029-000-00441-2	Lo Que Trabajo Necisita de las Escuelas	$3.25
	029-000-00437-4	Skills & Tasks for Jobs	$27.00
	029-000-00438-2	Teaching the SCANS Competencies	$11.00
		Total Cost of Order	

Prices include regular domestic postage and handling and are subject to change. International customers add 25%.

_____
(Company or Personal Name)   (Please type or print)

_____
(Additional address/attention line)

_____
(Street address)

_____
(City, State, ZIP Code)

_____
(Daytime phone including area code)

_____
(Purchase Order No.

Please Choose Method of Payment:

☐ Check Payable to the Superintendent of Documents

☐ GPO Deposit Account ☐☐☐☐☐☐☐–☐

☐ VISA or MasterCard Account

☐☐☐☐☐☐☐☐☐☐☐☐☐☐☐☐☐☐☐☐

☐☐☐☐ (Credit card expiration date)

Thank you for your order!

_____
(Authorizing Signature)   5/92

Mail To: Superintendent of Documents
P.O. Box 371954, Pittsburgh, PA 15250–7954

or order from your nearest Government Bookstore

U.S. Government Bookstores are located in the following cities: Atlanta, Denver, New York, Birmingham, Ala., Detroit, Philadelphia, Boston, Houston, Pittsburgh, Chicago, Jacksonville, Fla., Portland, Ore., Cleveland, Kansas City, Mo., Pueblo, Colo., Columbus, Laurel, Md., San Francisco, Dallas, Los Angeles, Seattle, Milwaukee and Washington, D.C. **(See your yellow pages.)**

Photocopies of this order form are acceptable.

- -

ISBN 0-16-037908-3